# Praise for *The Comeback*

"*The Comeback* surges across the past two thousand years of history with scholastic ease, reframing some of the current Aboriginal debates through an inspired lens … Saul lives up to his reputation for breadth and originality of thought … As in previous books, (Saul's) strength is to ground Canadian narratives in world history, presenting ideals that rise above the petty constraints of the day. *The Comeback* continues in this vein, as both a history of ideas and important polemic on what needs to be done. His is a hopeful vision." —*National Post*

"The most powerful indictment I've read by a non-aboriginal person of our ongoing indifference to Ottawa's refusal to settle 'the single biggest unresolved issue' of our time … Saul pricks your conscience so much that you pause often and think long and hard about how we, as citizens, are complicit." —Haroon Siddiqui, *Toronto Star*

"[Saul] has written a powerful treatise that provides a fresh way to look at Canadian history. It's important that native peoples have a writer of his heft in their corner." —*The Globe and Mail*

"If the biggest favour one human being can do another is to speak the truth, especially when that truth is uncomfortable to hear, then Canadians probably owe John Ralston Saul a collective nod of thanks." —Jim Coyle, *Toronto Star*

"*The Comeback* is a book that every Canadian should read. The book can assist in creating a dialogue between Aboriginal and non-Aboriginal Canadians within a context that is clear and creates a happy medium for all Canadians to start the dialogue our government is ignoring. This seems to be John Ralston Saul's guide to creating reconciliation in this Canada." —*Muskrat Magazine*

# Praise for *A Fair Country*

"A brilliant and timely argument about Canada's complex nature and our country's best future course. What a relief it is to read something so observant about Canada."     —*The Globe and Mail*

"There's something admirable, possibly even heroic, in the earnest anger of John Ralston Saul as he bangs away at the theme of his book, *A Fair Country*."     —*National Post*

"A stinging assessment of public and private sector leaders paralyzed by a 'colonial inferiority complex.'"     —*Edmonton Journal*

"Gutsy and exciting. It will start heated and overdue arguments … *A Fair Country* has the potential to change the way Canadians see themselves forever. It offers a romantic and heroic vision, and it's a stirring and unpretentious read."     —*Winnipeg Free Press*

"An excellent first step to recovery. By seriously examining aboriginal influences in Canadian history, Saul goes some way to curing the ongoing dysfunction suffered by—not Aboriginal Canadians—but by mainstream Canadians."     —*Calgary Herald*

"To anyone who recognizes the Anishnabek world view of Turtle Island, the [cover] illustration is a perfect summation of Saul's thesis. Canada is, indeed, a Métis nation. Saul's carefully constructed and illuminating argument offers us a new way of viewing ourselves … Our ties to the Aboriginal, Saul argues, are far stronger than our ties to the European. Clearly, this makes some more than a touch uncomfortable, even angry, which will certainly lead to good debate. And isn't that the point of a great book? … *A Fair Country* will change the way we view ourselves as a nation."
—Joseph Boyden, author of *The Orenda* and *Through Black Spruce*

"[Saul] fires an endless number of thought-salvoes, burns down ivory towers, and creates a whole new dimension of discourse."
—*The Gazette* (Montreal)

PENGUIN

# THE COMEBACK

JOHN RALSTON SAUL is Canada's leading public intellectual. Declared a "prophet" by *Time* magazine, Saul has received many awards and prizes, including Chile's Pablo Neruda Medal. He is president of PEN International, the leading global organization of writers dedicated to freedom of expression and literarure. He has published fourteen works, which have been translated into twenty-eight languages in thirty-seven countries, the most recent of which are *A Fair Country* and *Dark Diversions*.

## ALSO BY JOHN RALSTON SAUL

NON-FICTION

Voltaire's Bastards

The Doubter's Companion

The Unconscious Civilization

On Equilibrium

The Collapse of Globalism:
And the Reinvention of the World

Reflections of a Siamese Twin

A Fair Country: Telling Truths About Canada

Joseph Howe and the Battle for Freedom of Speech

Louis Hippolyte LaFontaine and Robert Baldwin

FICTION

The Birds of Prey

The Field Trilogy
I. Baraka or The Lives, Fortunes, and Sacred Honor
of Anthony Smith
II. The Next Best Thing
III. The Paradise Eater

Dark Diversions

# THE COMEBACK
## JOHN RALSTON SAUL

PENGUIN
an imprint of Penguin Canada Books Inc., a Penguin Random House Company

Published by the Penguin Group
Penguin Canada Books Inc., 90 Eglinton Avenue East, Suite 700, Toronto, Ontario, Canada M4P 2Y3

Penguin Group (USA) LLC, 375 Hudson Street, New York, New York 10014, U.S.A.
Penguin Books Ltd, 80 Strand, London WC2R 0RL, England
Penguin Ireland, 25 St Stephen's Green, Dublin 2, Ireland (a division of Penguin Books Ltd)
Penguin Group (Australia), 707 Collins Street, Melbourne, Victoria 3008, Australia
(a division of Pearson Australia Group Pty Ltd)
Penguin Books India Pvt Ltd, 11 Community Centre, Panchsheel Park, New Delhi – 110 017, India
Penguin Group (NZ), 67 Apollo Drive, Rosedale, Auckland 0632, New Zealand
(a division of Pearson New Zealand Ltd)
Penguin Books (South Africa) (Pty) Ltd, 24 Sturdee Avenue, Rosebank,
Johannesburg 2196, South Africa

Penguin Books Ltd, Registered Offices: 80 Strand, London WC2R 0RL, England

First published in Viking hardcover by Penguin Canada Books Inc., 2014
Published in this edition, 2015

1 2 3 4 5 6 7 8 9 10 (RRD)

Manufactured in the U.S.A.

LIBRARY AND ARCHIVES CANADA CATALOGUING IN PUBLICATION

Saul, John Ralston, 1947-, author
The comeback / John Ralston Saul.
Reprint. Originally published: Toronto : Viking, 2014.
Includes bibliographical references and index.

ISBN 978-0-14-319272-5 (pbk.)
1. Native peoples--Canada--Social conditions--21st century.
I. Title.

E78.C2S29 2015          971.004'97          C2015-903314-4

eBook ISBN 978-0-14-319315-9

Visit the Penguin Canada website at www.penguin.ca

Special and corporate bulk purchase rates available; please see
www.penguin.ca/corporatesales or call 1-800-810-3104.

For
Georges Erasmus
with admiration

# CONTENTS

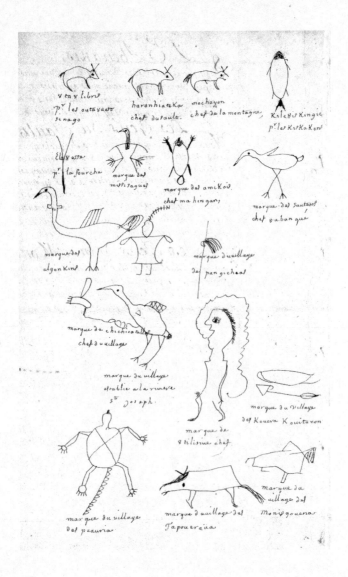

8 tag libre
p.r les outavacs
sinago

haranhiateko
chef du saulo

machayon
chef de la montagne

Kiledis Kingie
p.r les KisKa Kon

Ela 8 assa
p.r la fourche

marque das
misisague?

marque das amikois
chef ma hingan;

marque das sautaus
chef 8 abangue

marque das
algonKins

marque d'uillage
das pan gichras

marque de chichicatalli
chef du uillage

marque du uillage
establie a la riuieve
s.t Joseph.

marque de
8 tilimie chef

marque du uillage
das Koueva Kouitanon

marque du uillage
das peauria

marque d'uillage das
Tapoueraua

marque du
uillage das
Monisgouana

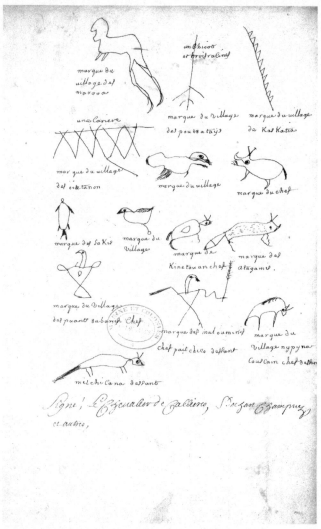

The Great Peace of Montreal, 1701. The signature page. This was a remarkable diplomatic agreement between oral and written cultures, but based on indigenous concepts. The Iroquois, forty other First Nations and New France all signed. Thirteen hundred delegates attended. This is the beginning of the Canadian idea of treaty.
© Library and Archives Canada, 3192491.

# I

# HISTORY IS UPON US

We know we live in history. We know we can shape it, although far less than we would like. And when we do intervene, it is inseparable from the great force with which history moves, surging across generations with ease. The full impact of that intervention – of getting it right or getting it wrong – is something that will slowly unfold over decades, even centuries. So history both constrains us and demands of us a great deal. Most of the time we can't see its shape and instead feel ourselves caught up in mysterious tides, unable to make out the great flow. Or perhaps we don't want to.

But we are always somewhere in history. Struggling in the waves. Being dashed on the rocks. Or just paddling innocently along.

The winter of 2012–13 needs to be thought of in these terms. Idle No More swept into our lives. Indigenous people massed in protest where protest was not expected, in shopping malls, at intersections across the country, as well as on Parliament Hill. New young leaders could be read and heard in all the media. The established leadership, non-Aboriginal and Aboriginal, the media, the experts tried without success to shape or control this organic expression of frustration and anger. Federal political leaders attended with solicitude at the side of Chief Theresa Spence, who was on a hunger strike on Victoria Island. Had she died from the effects of her liquid fast, within sight of the Parliament Buildings, a dangerous line would have been crossed. Irreparable damage would have been done to Canada's social fabric, her death a modern version of Riel's hanging. Events might then have slipped out of all control. Violence? We cannot know. In the end we stumbled out of the crisis. The governor general received the chiefs in a troubled atmosphere. There was a prime ministerial meeting to which some key chiefs refused to go unless the governor general was present.

The whole country seemed to be hypnotized by the seemingly abrupt arrival of indigenous people at the very centre of national consciousness. I say "seemingly" because the Canadian people and our government have not been paying attention. This was not just a rough patch in Aboriginal relations with the rest of Canada. It was not about personalities or a particular problem. It was not about Idle No More versus the Assembly of First Nations. Or various chiefs versus the national chief. Or those on hunger strikes versus those trying to negotiate. Each of those elements was part of a broad movement wrapped up in the forces of history. Then and now, Aboriginal and non-Aboriginal, each of us must try to fit the pieces together. Aboriginal people were at the very centre of national affairs because that is where they belong. They were at the centre of the national consciousness, as they should be, but in a way that reminded anyone willing to listen of what was and is at stake. This is the great issue of our time, the great unresolved Canadian question upon which history will judge us all.

Historic moments are always uncomfortable. They are always filled with strategic contradictions. Tactical contradictions. There are always divisions among those seeking more power for their cause. That is an almost necessary characteristic of movements seeking important social change. As for those in authority, they find themselves pulled and pushed in an atmosphere of crisis that melts the mechanical norms of power.

And so to those under attack – in this case the Canadian government and some of the non-Aboriginal leadership elements of Canadian society – it may seem that these divisions offer a cynical opportunity. To play one group of Aboriginals off against another. To attempt, for example, to discredit the Aboriginal leadership by attacking a handful of chiefs who overspend. Or a bit of corruption here. Or ineffectiveness there. Anything to avoid addressing real, long-standing questions. Or to avoid resolving real problems. But these are false opportunities. A false reading of what is happening.

Clever tactics or stalling won't make the situation go away and will resolve nothing. Most important, without a serious level of resolution, the fundamental flaws in this relationship will simply become more troubling for all of us and increasingly problematic for the existence of Canada.

This historic reality is not helped by the natural tendency of the media and of political backrooms to view their own reality through the details of the day. It is natural. And it is necessary. They are endlessly drilling down – as they see it – into personalities, rivalries, divisions, failures. This is how they perceive their job – examining the entrails of chickens in order to tell us whether Caesar ought to go to the Forum.

This can also become a problem when dealing with a crisis, particularly a long-standing crisis. We are all caught up in the established narrative of the day. And within that narrative each of us is focused on our own particular realities. Our own habits, practical and emotional. This is normal. And in normal times it may work. But the key to dealing with a real crisis, one that goes beyond our personal realities, lies in our ability to move outside what we think of as normal. If the crisis is big enough, we have to reconsider the narrative or we can be destroyed by it. For example, during the crisis, the prime minister, Mr. Harper, usually locked fast onto an economic narrative of whatever is going on. A very particular economic interpretation at that. Such is his reality. As for Canadians at large, we have myriad realities. Some of them are as simple as getting to work on time or having access to gas for our cars. Anything that gets in the way annoys us. We have thousands of ambitions and concerns involving our families, our employment, our lives.

On broader social issues, we tend to focus on any sign of suffering. We are troubled by suffering, by the suffering of others. That is a classic Judeo-Christian – let's say Abrahamic – expression of empathy. Not a bad thing. It is a good emotive entry level into public dramas. But if non-Aboriginals define their relationship to the Aboriginal reality through their emotions, well then, this emotional drama may simply take the place of ensuring that the issues are dealt with. That kind of sympathy may simply reinforce the old narrative in which "Indians" are a problem and unsuited to survival in "modern" society because they have been so shamed by us as to have lost the self-confidence necessary to function in the real world. Lee Maracle, in a conversation with CBC Radio host Michael Enright on May 18, 2014, offered a sharp correction to this destructive sympathy. "Shame is what other people call it. No one says it about themselves." In this case, if there is shame it should be felt by the perpetrators. Maracle: "For any reconciliation to take place, the party that hurt you has to take part."

Whatever our personal approach to reality, history is still at work. When we do try to work out exactly where we are in that history, well, it is not much more than a guess. History is always moving in various directions and at various speeds at the same time. It is filled with undertows and treacherous riptides.

Yet it does seem to me that right now we can see at least one pattern. And although it is one among many, I believe that not only our individual lives but Canada itself will be shaped by how we respond to it. If we engage intelligently, consciously and with a sense of the direction of our history, we will be able to change our narrative. By that I mean we will free ourselves from a surprisingly colonial narrative and embrace one that makes sense of what we do and can do in this place. The pattern is clear. For the last hundred years, Aboriginal peoples have been making a comeback – a remarkable comeback from a terrifyingly low point. A low point of population, of legal respect, of civilizational stability. A comeback to what? To a position of power, influence and civilizational creativity in the territory we call Canada.

Most Canadians still don't understand this because we are focused on the suffering of many indigenous people, the problems, the failures. This leads some non-Aboriginals to feel guilt, others to sympathize, still others to write off the various Aboriginal societies as failed civilizations. These are roughly the same three responses as a century ago, except that the guilt and sympathy quotients are much higher and the dismissal quotient much lower. But all three are essentially negative and distract us from the main flow of history. And from our obligations.

What I mean is that our three responses distract us from the reality that most of the problems faced by Aboriginal peoples are solvable. And our pessimism – our guilt, sympathy and dismissal – blocks these perfectly achievable resolutions. Aboriginal peoples are in the process of solving them. We are still getting in the way.

The situation is simple. Aboriginals have made and will continue to make a remarkable comeback. They cannot be stopped. Non-Aboriginals have a choice to make. We can continue to stand in the way so that the comeback is slowed and surrounded by bitterness. Or we can be supportive and part of a new narrative.

Early in the twentieth century, First Nations and Métis reached the bottom of their population collapse. From as many as two million people they had melted down over some seventy-five years to approximately one hundred and fifty thousand. It was a vertiginous plunge, brought on by the loss of their ways of life, of their economic well-being, of their social well-being and of their food sources, as well as the rise of yet another wave of European diseases, this one particularly destructive, in good part because of their physically weakened condition. And all this was driven along its way by, or was a direct result of, government policy, continuing immigration and the resulting change in the use of land.

In other words, here was a period of deep contradictions in the reality and the mythology of Canadian life. Our standard national history portrays the turn of the nineteenth into the twentieth century as an era of creativity and nation building. The levels of immigration remain unmatched to this day. In the decade before World War I they grew to over four hundred thousand a year. Land was broken. Towns built. Railways were in permanent expansion, spurs off in every direction as villages grew into towns. All true. But at exactly the same time, in the same country, indigenous peoples were dying or suffering or not reproducing because of the terrible conditions to which they had been reduced, and doing most of this in small communities, out of the sight and mind of the largely European Canadian population.

As the indigenous population collapsed, the Canadian political system, emboldened by increasing numbers and power, declared the end to be nigh. It was clear – or so the common, self-serving argument went – that these native populations were unfortunately unsuited to the modern world. Backward. Weak. Stuck in irrelevant cultures. Much of this argument was folded into standard Victorian, imperial, Christian notions of charity.

It was the era of overwhelming empire mythologies. Around the world the imperial power and imperial myths of a handful of countries dominated all thoughts and actions. Few of us today have any real sense of just how powerful and truly international these imperial mythologies were. They were also astonishingly parochial. After all, they asserted that little countries with small populations like Britain and France should set the pattern for the world. Charles Darwin's theories of evolution, revealed to the world in 1859, were quickly mangled into a populist political narrative, filled with strange leaps of logic. For example, it was assumed that because things had happened over thousands of years, setting a painfully slow pattern of evolution, whatever was done today by those capable of taking power was actually a manifestation of scientific destiny. And scientific destiny somehow meant that these changes were intentional. So, in yet another remarkable leap, the altering of an insect's wing by a fraction of a millimetre over thousands of years was equated with the immediate political destiny of empires and the racial superiority of those

Francis Pegahmagabow (1891–1952), third generation chief of the Wasauksing First Nation on Georgian Bay. Most successful allied sniper of World War I. Three times awarded the Military Medal. In 1943 Supreme Chief of the Native Independent Government. Photographed in June 1945 while in Ottawa. Canadian Museum of History, 95293.

who ran them. The victories of European armies outside Europe somehow signalled that the winners were the carriers of Darwinian destiny. They were intended to lead the world in everything from table manners and dress codes to economic methods, political philosophy and governmental administration. In his remarkable book of ideas, *Principles of Tsawalk*, E. Richard Atleo (Umeek) eloquently describes and analyzes how Darwin was used against indigenous peoples. The Darwinian "theory of evolution and its interpretations created, for colonizers, a view of differences between people that was and is characterized by superiority and inferiority."

It is essential in this situation simply to put aside the serious aspects of Darwin and look at how his ideas were quickly jumbled up with those of others into a political ideology of evolution, progress and race that justified whatever the Western empires wanted to do. Darwin's "natural selection" became by 1864, thanks to the pen of Herbert Spencer, "the survival of the fittest." Suddenly public debate was full of scientific truisms that were neither scientific nor true. Natural selection was somehow a reason for colonial wars. Evolutionary biology became an excuse for any kind of organized racism. The preservation of favoured races in the struggle for life was an explanation for empire. By the 1870s we had social Darwinism.

All of this would lead to Hitler's murderous racial theories. We all know about the violence, the inhumanity, the tragedy. But we should never forget that the theories were simply nonsense. And make no mistake, the British, French and American empires were built on that same social Darwinist ideology. Nor should we forget that in the second half of the nineteenth century, Canadian Aboriginal policy was deformed by social Darwinism and so became a creature of its time.

Why did so few people see how horrible all of this was? One explanation is that it was woven seamlessly into our concepts of progress and democracy. Rank racism was institutionalized within the fundamentals of European philosophy and culture. No break with rationality or the Enlightenment or individualism was required, nor, I repeat, with progress and democracy. What's more, all these elements remain in place today.

Europeans insisted that their principles were universal. Of course they were universal. After all, they said they were. They still say it, with the same old conviction.

All around the world today you can be served slices of tasteless white toast or equally tasteless baguettes. The details of universality as mediocrity are always fascinating – think of them as the lingering crumbs of massive international forces. They make sense because just behind them lie the imperial national schools of philosophy, which are still anchored around the world in their universities, and in ours, and taught as universal. Their national narrative of history, of civilization, of cuisine, of fashion, all apparently universal.

One of the biggest barriers to reconciliation between Aboriginals and non-Aboriginals in Canada is precisely the continuing power of these narratives in our universities. And, it follows, in how we imagine that a state must function. The power of narrative is absolute.

Today's mythologies of globalization and economic determinism are small-time and regional compared with these ideologies of civilizational truth and destiny. The tattered remnants of English exceptionalism and French exceptionalism, the century of American exceptionalism, all of these remain inextricably linked to this warped idea of a Darwinian destiny.

At first glance such overwhelming imperial power did indeed seem to be justified by Western nations' technological leadership, military prowess and cultural sophistication. But the key intellectual tool – and the central mythological tool – was the conviction of racial superiority. Racism. It was all about white people, pink people, at the top. This was God's team, with Darwinian determinism and the machinery of modernism on its side.

In only a few years these intellectually and politically argued myths, laid out with detail and with great self-confidence, would lead the European peoples to massacre themselves in first one world war and then a second. The result was a continental civil war lasting thirty-two years and fought over their theories of race and governance. It was clinically delusional behaviour, the outcome of four centuries of European determinism. And yes, the European outliers like the Canadians, Indians, Algerians, Australians and New Zealanders, along with a multitude of other non-European servants of the empires, would be drawn into the argument. One hundred million dead in less than half a century. A historic record. And all in the name of Western superiority. It is always fascinating how delusion comes with self-justifying, even enabling parameters. The United States went in as the smallest of the European-style empires and came out as the new Rome with its own version of saving civilization, because Americans, like those who had come before, were driven by their exceptionalism. It's peculiar to go back and read what London, Paris, Berlin, Washington, Rome, Brussels, Amsterdam and yes, the outliers in places like Ottawa were saying about race to justify their actions in the lead-up years to the wars. Educational curricula were filled with these absurdities.

It was in the forty years before the European civil war began that Canadians of European origin decided that "Indians," "Half-breeds" and "Esquimaux" were among the destined losers when faced by our superiority – our Darwinian destiny. And so we set about helping them on their way to oblivion, banning languages, cultures, rituals. Of course, it was more complicated than that. In a country that believed it was built on the rule of law, respectable mechanisms had to be put in place. Myriad laws, regulations and administrative structures were created and amended in order to install a legal infrastructure of racism and punishment, both social and economic. Residential schools were only one part. But they were an important initiative because a boarding school system gave the state, through the churches, total control over future generations. Behind the progressive mask of education, using the key mechanisms of civilizations – language, culture and all things spiritual – they could mount a direct attack on indigenous peoples. The sexual exploitation, the medical malpractice, the experimentation – all could be seen as expressions of the European racial desire to demean other races. Perhaps these acts of evil betray a desperate innate desire to convince themselves that their racial ideology of superiority was true.

Am I exaggerating? Here is Prime Minister John A. Macdonald speaking in the House of Commons in 1883. He is explaining the need for residential schools: "When the school is on the reserve, the child lives with his parents who are savages; he is surrounded by savages, and though he may learn to read and write, his habits and training and mode of thought are Indian. He is simply a savage who can read and write." These words from our first post-Confederation prime minister clarify the issue. We are dealing with deeply rooted, European-style racism that is central to the late-nineteenth-century narrative.

On the West Coast, the banning of the potlatch ceremonies was dressed up as a reform to protect the economic wealth and moral well-being of the natives. It was actually an attempt to weaken those natives who had adjusted successfully to the newcomers' economic system and made themselves powerful players in the new fishing industry. At the national level, we took away their right to vote, to retain lawyers, to organize politically. The 1927 amendments to the Indian Act not only banned potlatches but made it virtually illegal to pursue land claims, and even illegal to wear Aboriginal clothing or perform traditional dances outside of any individual's own reserve. We broke our own laws by pretending that "Indians" could not leave their reserves without the permission of the local government official: a fiction made up by senior civil servants in the Department of Indian Affairs. And, of course, we broke the treaties that had been signed in good faith by the Aboriginal side, and in earlier periods in good faith by both sides.

Remember, we non-Aboriginals were signatories. As a non-Aboriginal, I say *we*. And through Canada's signatures we committed ourselves to the permanency of our relationship with the words that these treaties would stand "as long as the sun shines, the grass grows and the river flows." These were and remain binding legal documents. Perhaps more important, with our signatures we committed our government to act always with the *Honour of the Crown*.

The illegal, immoral, unethical acts that followed represented far more than the breaking of specific treaties. We were betraying relationships that were based on good faith and to which Aboriginals made immeasurable contributions. Aboriginals understood these actions as a betrayal of those properly established and maintained relationships. They laid this out in thousands of letters, petitions and written speeches. One of the most eloquent summaries of the situation was the letter presented by British Columbian chiefs of the interior – Chief Petit Louis of the Secwépemc, Chief John Tetlenitsa of the Nlaka'pamux and Chief John Chilahitsa of the Syilx – to Prime Minister Wilfrid Laurier at a meeting in the Oddfellows Hall in Kamloops on August 25, 1910, during his historic tour of Canada by rail. Over the years, the arguments of the indigenous – these were far more than protests – were developed into a complex intellectual and legal framework built up on the foundation of treaties and civilizational arrangements stretching back to the beginnings of New France, the Great Peace of Montreal of 1701, the Royal Proclamation of 1763 and the Treaty of Fort Niagara of 1764.

So the indigenous–immigrant relationship was carefully developed over hundreds of years and largely in good faith. What followed from the 1870s on was quite different. Increasingly, non-Aboriginals did not act in good faith. And each of these betrayals we undertook in order to help them disappear. For their own good.

Most of us believe that we are now free of these attitudes. We condemn them. But it isn't as simple as that. To free ourselves, two things must happen. We must reinstall a national narrative built upon the centrality of the Aboriginal peoples' past, present and future. And the policies of the country must reflect that centrality, both conceptually and financially.

# II

# RIGHTS, NOT SYMPATHY

All of this must be said, and said repeatedly; otherwise, those Canadians who do not think of themselves as Aboriginal will go on misleading themselves as to what is now happening. They will misread the movement of history, the meaning of the events we are all living, the possibility of a reimagined narrative.

What is happening today is not about guilt or sympathy or failure. It is not about a romantic view of the past. Nor about old ways versus new ways. Nor about propping up people who can't make it on their own.

What we face is a simple matter of rights – of citizens' rights that are still being denied to indigenous peoples. It is a matter of rebuilding relationships central to the creation of Canada and, equally important, to its continued existence. But there is more. We also face the possibility of those relationships opening up a more creative and accurate way of imagining ourselves. A different narrative.

Getting the narrative right is so important that I want to repeat the argument about what stands in the way. If we are not careful, informed and conscious, we can easily slip back into passive forms of sympathy when confronted with the suffering of First Nations children or poverty on reserves or family problems coming out of the destructive effects of the residential schools or failures in leadership. This is not an honest reaction. This is the modern shape of deeply ingrained attitudes going back to those old European-derived attitudes of superiority.

I have never heard of Aboriginal peoples seeking to be categorized as victims. I often feel that, when it comes to Aboriginal peoples, sympathy from outsiders is the new form of racism. It allows many of us to feel good about discounting their importance and the richness of their civilizations.

Sympathy is a way to deny our shared reality. Our shared responsibility. Sympathy obscures the central importance of rights.

If not sympathy, then what? In September 2013, in the Columbia River Basin, I listened to Kathryn Teneese, chair of the Ktunaxa Nation Council, explain that the first step is "recognition and acknowledgment." Then we can work at our relationship "one step at a time – and gradually – find things we can do together." In other words, "reconciliation" is not an event. It is not an apology, although an apology was neces-sary. And it is certainly not something so lacking in respect and dignity as sympathy. In any case, no solid relationship is possible so long as the Canadian government continues to rise in courtrooms and begin cases against the rights of Aboriginal nations by first arguing before the law that they do not exist as a people. This is our government. What could sympathy possibly mean if it is preceded by a denial of existence? In the same already mentioned conversation involving Lee Maracle and Michael Enright, Taiaiake Alfred argued that reconcili-ation can mean something if it starts from the position of restitution.

The poet, Lee Maracle, and the philosopher, Taiaiake Alfred. Two powerful voices. © *MUSKRAT* Magazine.

On the prairies there is an important piece of formal rhetoric: a question and an answer widely used in public meetings in order to remind everyone present of the reality in which they live.

"Who are the treaty people?"

"We are the treaty people."

Treaties are signed by two parties. Both are bound by their signatures. Equally bound. Canada is built on and by the treaties, going right back to the first oral agreement made in the summer of 1609 between the Maliseet, the Montagnais, the Algonquin and the French on the low-tide sands of the Saguenay opposite Tadoussac. And Canada is built not only on the legal structure of the treaties, but equally on the cultural, ethical, human assumptions and commitments those treaties contain. These were and are the commitments of both indigenous peoples and newcomers entering into permanent community relationships. In fact, the treaties are in good part about newcomers entering into both the concept and the social reality of the indigenous circle. What does that mean?

Well, not all societies function in the same way. We are used to the European presumption that there may well be small, valid differences between serious civilizations – different social protocols, for example, different forms of politeness, of negotiation and so on. But these involve mere tweaks on the basic – there they are again – *universal* assumptions, all of which have been defined in Europe or in the Western tradition.

Powerful societies, imperial societies and their outlying imitators find it very difficult to admit that there can be fundamentally different models. That these other models not only work, but could be just as valid and might even have real advantages over the imperial model. And that while ultimate ideas of, for example, ethics may be shared across these models, how you get there, the use and avoidance of violence, and how you relate to the environment – to take just three examples – may be very different.

Platonist-dominated societies, like the European, see humans as the purpose of the planet and constantly seek conclusive answers that suit those humans. They lean toward the Manichaean. Lots of right versus wrong. Lots of moral determinism. This seems to go well with the idea of continual progress. A very linear idea. It leads down a path into such simple utilitarian assertions as "continual growth." Again, very linear.

Asian societies have a variety of very different models. For most of the last couple of thousand years, methods such as the

Confucian have outperformed Western approaches. For the last three hundred years the Western method has outperformed those of the East. The last two decades have seen a messy, often ugly but nevertheless powerful return of those Eastern theories. The West has done its best to pretend that China's economic success, for example, is the result of its adopting Western methods. This simply isn't true. Western technology has been used, but very little of Western theory. For better and for worse. The theory that has driven Chinese economics has far more to do with the elite version of Confucianism and the Chinese version of Communist initiative.

What about indigenous societies? Well, it could be argued that in the northern half of North America these tend to take a spatial or circular approach. What does that mean? Humans are part of the whole, not elevated above the place and its other inhabitants. And so humans see themselves from within existence. They do not gaze down upon it from above. This changes radically how things are conceived and therefore how things could be done. What does this mean in practical terms today?

Let's take the example of the environment. Most of us agree that we are in some sort of environmental crisis, brought on in good part by a Western model that removes all effective philosophical brakes on human activity by interpreting the planet as our passive servant. Ours is a civilization built on a philosophy that involves no real brakes on movement. That has been a great strength. It accounts for many of our break-throughs and our capacity to build in so many ways and to accumulate wealth. But it also accounts for the ease with which we slip into violence and, today, for our incapacity to take the environmental crisis seriously. Suddenly, our unflinching commitment to an idea of progress, which requires continual movement, begins to resemble a wilful child out of control – destructive and self-destructive. More and more people see ours as an old-fashioned, even dangerous theory. On the other hand, the northern indigenous philosophy sees the human as an integral part of the whole. Which means that we all have obligations to the other elements of existence. This could now be described as an appropriate, even as a highly contemporary philosophical, model for all of us. For a good explanation of this, read Richard Atleo's *Principles of Tsawalk*, which I referred to earlier.

These very different civilizational concepts were shared to some extent by Europeans within Europe until the early seventeenth century. What's more, the Europeans who came to the northern half of North America from 1600 on rapidly came to accept and live within the First Nations' philosophical view. Why? Well, partly because these newcomers came from societies not yet dominated by "modern" linear concepts. What's more, they were weaker than the indigenous peoples, dependent on them, partners with them. To put it simply: most things were organized around the First Nations' point of view. And it worked. It made sense to most newcomers because they saw it as a way to survive. I wrote a great deal about this in *A Fair Country*.

And so, from the beginning, treaty negotiations and the treaties themselves reflected the indigenous world view. The Great Peace of Montreal (1701) and the Treaty of Niagara (1764) are two fundamental examples of this. Long after the colonial and then Canadian officials had ceased to believe in this indigenous approach to life, treaty negotiations and even treaties continued to reflect them. This was the way the later treaties were obtained: by pretending to believe in order to get the First Nations leaders to sign. Officials became increasingly hypocritical and cynical. No doubt an increasing number of the negotiators, representing Ottawa from the time of Confederation on, thought they could negotiate and sign in bad faith. In their minds there was only one model – European – and so these treaties were simple tools of power involving a transfer in ownership of land.

But the legal texts are just that. Legal commitments. And their meaning as complex, people-to-people treaties was reinforced by the government negotiators' oral explanations of those texts during the negotiations, as well as by the Aboriginal negotiators' explanations of their own understanding of the agreements being put in place. All of these elements were made clear in public before anything was signed. And so all parties agreed publicly that their relationships were to continue as always understood. These were permanent nation-to-nation agreements with obligations on both sides. To this the governmental negotiators committed the Crown legally, ethically and morally. And over the last four decades that reality has led the Supreme Court to rule repeatedly in favour of the Aboriginal position and against that of Ottawa, the provinces and the private sector.

Anyone sworn in as a Canadian citizen today or tomorrow inherits the full benefits and the full responsibilities – the obligations – of those treaties. British Columbia is only very marginally an exception to this reality, because it has signed fewer treaties. But the Douglas Treaties of 1850–1854 were among the most clearly tied to the Canadian tradition. And now British Columbia is slowly but surely entering into the treaty reality of Canada with such breakthroughs as the Nisga'a

Treaty of 1999. The number of crucial Aboriginal victories at the Supreme Court coming out of B.C. is remarkable.

The change in northern Quebec is even more dramatic. Into the 1970s Ottawa and Quebec City acted like colonial potentates. In 1972 Premier Bourassa walked out on a Cree delegation led by Malcolm Diamond, saying he couldn't be bothered. Three years later he accepted reality with the James Bay Agreement, respecting Inuit rights. The Cree, betrayed, fought back, with leaders like Malcolm Diamond's son, Billy.

It took twenty years. Eventually the courts ruled against Quebec, thus endangering the provincial forestry industry. Premier Landry, faced by reality, sat down with the Cree, led by Ted Moses. Twelve months later they had an agreement. *Le Paix des Braves*. Revolutionary in speed and content.

Why revolutionary in content? Because Cree treaty rights were not extinguished. What then did Canada or Quebec lose? Nothing. Why then does Ottawa still insist that negotiations require the extinguishing of treaty rights? Because they use the European monolithic model of legitimacy. But Canada is more complicated than that. As the Cree negotiator, Romeo Saganash, puts it, *indigenous people are one of the components of the country's sovereignty*. To embrace multiple sovereignties is to show strength. Everyone benefits.

Yet Ottawa persists with its colonial model which opens the door to every negative possibility. Our governments continue to oppose restitution and serious reconciliation. Those who have been ignored and insulted for more than a century have every reason to lose patience. Why lose yet another generation while Canada plays games? Increasingly, they have enough power to abandon patience as the primary tactical card of a minority under attack.

# III

# WORKING TO AVOID JUSTICE

Again, what does all of this mean in practical terms?
When you learn that almost half of First Nations children live in poverty, that the federal government spends less on the education of each First Nations child than provincial governments spend on each non–First Nations child, you are not only learning of a reason to be ashamed. You are also learning that the Canadian government – the power of each of us as citizens – has been and still is breaking the law. Breaking it by misusing it – by resorting to avoidance, by pretending to be doing what it isn't, by legalistic and administrative manipulation, by malingering. These are standard tricks far beneath the dignity of the Crown. For example, the federal government is not fulfilling its education obligations under the Nunavut Treaty. As a result, Ottawa is now defending itself in the courts. Dragging things out, playing the legalistic corners as if they were disreputable lawyers defending dubious figures. Why spend public money in a good cause, to which you previously committed, when you can spend much more public money arguing in order to avoid fulfilling your obligations?

True, there was an attempt in 2014 to pass through Parliament a major First Nations education bill. But its introduction of provincial authority through provincial standards under-standably divided the indigenous community. That is the core of the complaint that there was not proper consultation. The seemingly neutral concept of provincial standards actually suggests the elimination of indigenous culture in favour of the old "universal" model. This has already created a terrible problem in the education system of Nunavut, where the Alberta Department of Education has been involved in setting standards that undermine Inuit culture.

And the shuffling off of federal education responsibility to the provinces can be interpreted as an indirect way of under-mining Canada's treaty obligations.

This adds to the sense that our government is still breaking our treaty obligations. If you coolly strip away the endless administrative rhetoric about budgets and governance, the endless studies and the endemic lack of broad policies coming from the Department of Indian Affairs, you begin to realize that we are still caught up in the racist assimilation policies of a century ago.

Let me take a broader example. We all know that the treaties involved a massive loss of land for First Nations. What most of us pretend we don't know is that this remark-able generosity was tied to permanent obligations taken on by colonial officials, then by the Government of Canada; that is, by the Crown; that is, by you and me. So we got the use of land – and therefore the possibility of creating Canada – in return for a relationship in which we have permanent obliga-tions. We have kept the land. We have repeatedly used ruses to get more of their land. And we have not fulfilled our side of the agreement. We pretend that we do not have partner-ship obligations. It's pretty straightforward. We criticize. We insult. We complain. We weasel. *Surely*, we say, *these handouts have gone on long enough*. But the most important handout was to us. Bob Rae put it this way at the Athabasca Chipewyan First Nation Treaty Conference in June 2014: "It's ridiculous to think people would say: 'I have all this land, millions and millions and millions of acres of land, I'm giving it to you for a piece of land that is five miles by five miles and a few dollars a year.' To put it in terms of a real estate transaction, it's preposterous. It doesn't make any sense." So the generosity was from First Nations to newcomers. And we are keeping that handout – the land – offered in good faith by friends and allies.

Many of today's negotiations or renegotiations involve one First Nation or another attempting to re-establish the treaty

Concerned that Chief Spence's fast might end in death, Bob Rae visited her on Victoria Island, on the Ottawa River, in sight of Parliament.
© Frank Gunn/The Canadian Press.

terms. Often this involves re-establishing their rights over land they never ceded – usually land in the interior, land in the north. Look at the Nisga'a negotiation. The federal government dragged it out for twenty-five years. And then, when it was finally done, the government of British Columbia tried to reopen the agreement. What had the Nisga'a got through the treaty? A small percentage of the land they had once held. What did our governments want? More. What did the British Columbian government want? Even more. Why? Well, when it comes to Aboriginal land, our governments always want more. Our corporations want more. Effectively, we all want more. This is our system of governance.

To be precise, you and I pay government lawyers to fight as hard as they can to get as much Aboriginal land as possible and to give as little as possible in return. They act like rapacious divorce lawyers.

Why? We must ask ourselves why they are doing this for us.

First, our governments seem to be arguing that these negotiations are all about saving the taxpayer money. This is lunacy. You don't save money by dragging out complex legal negotiations for twenty-five years. Protracted legal battles are the equivalent of throwing taxpayers' money away. And you force Canadian citizens – Aboriginals – to waste their own money and their lives on unnecessary battles.

Second, our governments more or less argue that a few thousand or a few hundred Aboriginals shouldn't have control over land that might have great timber or mineral or energy value. They argue as if it were all about the interests of a few thousand Aboriginals versus that of millions of Canadians. As if the Aboriginals were invaders come to steal our land.

The question we should be asking is quite different. If there is value in these territories, don't you want it controlled by Canadians who feel strongly that this is their land? By people who want to live there and want their children and grand-children to live there? Surely they are the people most likely to do a good long-term job at managing the land. And why shouldn't they profit from it? Wouldn't that be a good thing? Is there any reason why Canadians living in the interior and in the north should profit less than urban Canadians do in the south? And if those Canadians are Aboriginal, is there some reason why they should profit less than non-Aboriginals?

The only other option we have is for the government to hand control of the land to a dozen directors of a corporation sitting in Toronto or New York with no long-term interest. They simply want to extract the minerals or timber, extract the wealth from the land, and move on. That is the business they are in. You don't hear anyone argue that these tiny groups should make less profit. They are more admired by the market if they make more profit. So why wouldn't we admire Aboriginals for doing the same? Or, to put it another way, wouldn't we all benefit if those corporations had to deal every day with indigenous locals who are devoted to that land and have power over it?

Isn't there a risk, you wonder, of indigenous leaders being corrupted by the big corporations? No doubt. But aren't we already living with the problem of government officials, politicians, civil servants, political parties and mayors being corrupted by these companies or – to put it in gentler terms – agreeing to act in a compliant manner? They turn a blind eye to pollution risks. They spend years denying health risks. All in the name of development, growth and job creation opportunities.

Look at the history of asbestos. Is this not a story of public corruption? And today our government is selling this known toxic substance out in the world as if it doesn't know what it knows. Meanwhile the northern two-thirds of Canada is littered with the remains of abandoned mines. Toxic barrels. Tailing ponds. The companies are long gone. Or, if the government inadvertently catches up with them, they declare bankruptcy and take their money elsewhere. Only the taxpayer remains to clean up these sites. So the problem of political, administrative and corporate corruption is well and truly with us already. And the government has an obligation to get on top of it through stricter standards and regulations and the development of a culture of rigorous enforcement.

Frankly, few urban Canadians want to take personal responsibility for these millions of hectares in the interior and in the north. They don't want to live there. Shouldn't those of us who live in the cities in the south be grateful that indigenous peoples want to take on that responsibility?

Why do our governments continue to work so hard to prevent this happening, fighting hectare by hectare, dragging their feet? Why don't they want Aboriginal people to be successful and prosperous? Why are they so determined to maintain a paternalistic relationship?

# IV

# AUTHORITY VERSUS POWER

What I am describing is not the fault of one government or another. You get a sense of how profound the problem is when you look back at the recent crisis and the insistence of the chiefs and of Idle No More on the importance of the governor general. Most Canadians were confused by this because they think the problem is one of government policy – of politics – and have lost a clear sense of how the governor general fits in. Is he part of the political process? A figurehead? Ceremonial? The answer is that the governor general is meant to be above politics.

Many non-Aboriginals thought that this desire for the presence of the effective head of state meant that there was something romantic going on – an impossible hankering after the past. They were wrong.

Most Canadians were not listening carefully to what Aboriginals were saying. Aboriginals were not surprised. The problem for more than a century has been that non-Aboriginals seem to have lost the ability to listen to exactly what is being said by indigenous peoples. We find it troubling, or simply not what we want to hear.

What's more, many of us have forgotten, to the extent we have tried to understand, how our system of government actually works. We are not helped by politicians or journalists or, increasingly, academics who talk of government only in terms of power – either political or administrative – as if only power matters.

Power is certainly important, particularly in dictatorships, in places where constitutions, laws, unwritten rules, traditions and understandings don't count. But in a healthy democracy, power is a surprisingly limited element. And the unwritten conventions, understandings, forms of respect for how things are done, for how citizens relate to government and to each other, are surprisingly important. Why? Because if democracy is only power, then what we are left with is a system of deep distrust. Why? Because if only power matters – even if it is the result of an election – then the government feels that it has a mandate to do whatever it wants; that the law is there principally to serve power. If democracy is only about winning power and using it, then it has been deformed into a denial of society and of the idea of responsible citizenship.

And that is the increasingly common characteristic of government, even in democracies. Only power matters. This is partly the outcome of government being de-intellectualized. Elections are now thought to be unsuitable moments for real debates over ideas. In between these elections the focus is on administrative problems – legalistic, managerial undertakings. In this case, real debates over ideas are unnecessary because the decision about power was taken on election night. There is nothing, therefore, to debate. Worse still, the efficient putting in place of programs to be administered can only be made inefficient by debate.

And so we are witnessing a growth in the Napoleonic or Mussolinian corporatist idea that when citizens vote in an

election, it is actually an all-purpose referendum or plebiscite. It is then the winner's job to get on with running things.
First win an election, then administer as you wish. Omnibus
bills are one of the ways you can speed things up; they are a
great way to convert the deeply inefficient process of democracy, with all its thinking, debating and complex differences
of opinion, into a sort of shop-floor system of utilitarian efficiency. Therefore, once elected, a government has broad,
unlimited permission. Of course, during the Napoleonic era,
or even the Mussolinian era, managerialism was in its early
days. Today our universities are dominated by management
schools. The manager is to today's society what the lawyer
once was, or before that the military officer and the priest. If
you were to compare these four occupations by their qualities
of education, of social purpose, of acting as agents of change,
the profile of the manager would certainly rate below that of
the lawyer, probably that of the priest and in many ways that
of the officer. All things considered, the amorality of managerialism is more dangerous than the tension between morality
and immorality, which is more typical of the legal, priestly
and officer castes. In any case, today's plebiscitary approach is
both populist and anti-democratic. What it amounts to is this:
*We won the election. We have power. It is now a matter of administrative
efficiency. We can do what we want.*

No, you can't. There are treaties. There is a Constitution.
Just as important, there is an unwritten constitution. There
are unwritten rules. This is worth restating. These rules,
these structures, these understandings, written or unwritten,
are just as important as simple power. Often they are much
more important because power doesn't last long and lacks the
complexity of real societies.

Canada is now the oldest continuous democratic federation in the world, in good part because most of our leaders, and certainly the best ones, have respected most of these written and unwritten rules. Other countries – almost all our allies and friends – have suffered civil wars, coups, dictatorships, sharp breaks, because they could not maintain the flexibility and respect for *the Other* that these rules, in particular the unwritten rules, create.

As I began arguing in 1997 in *Reflections of a Siamese Twin*, one of our unwritten realities is that the country is built upon a triangular foundation – Aboriginal, francophone, anglophone. The ease with which Canada embraces diversity today has been made possible by our non-monolithic foundation. And that foundation worked to the extent it did largely because of the more complex ideas of belonging and identity in Aboriginal societies. What we call multiculturalism or interculturalism is constructed, and works because it is constructed, on those ideas. This isn't about population numbers or financial numbers or race or power. Without that underlying complexity we would have found ourselves in the European nightmare – the delusional myth of *one blood, one race, one people.* And so if you undermine the complexity of our foundation, you undermine diversity as the Canadian model.

Now let me go back to the role of the governor general. If you look at how the country functions, you see that there has always been a clear difference between authority and power. This is partly written, partly unwritten. The governor general represents authority. The prime minister, through Parliament, represents power. Authority is the expression of profound legitimacy. In Aboriginal terms this is the authority and legitimacy represented in part by elders. We call this the legitimacy of the Crown or the state. The Crown is the people. The people are the guarantors of the state. The governor general is the protector of the Crown; that is, of the people. This is not about money or law or soldiers. It is about a role above power, a concept of the state above interests.

This concept, in various forms, has been adopted by almost all democracies: a head of the state separated from the head of the executive, the voice of authority separated from the voice of power. Head of state is a full-time, on-the-ground job. It is an approach with deep historic roots, yet it now seems to be particularly appropriate and almost postmodern.

And so, in the Canadian version, a meeting between the prime minister and the national chief is a meeting about power. A meeting with the governor general present automatically invokes the state, the Crown, the people. And the Crown automatically invokes *the Honour of the Crown*, a concept given its Canadian form in such historic Supreme Court decisions as Guerin in 1984, Sparrow in 1990 and, most recently, the Manitoba Métis case in 2013.

The Guerin case is one of those Aboriginal victories at the highest court that have shaped Canada over the last forty years. What is the Honour of the Crown? It is the obligation of the state to act ethically in its dealings with the people. Not just legally or legalistically. Not merely administratively or efficiently. But ethically. The Honour of the Crown is the obligation of the state to act with respect for the citizen.

And so the presence or role of the governor general in a meeting involving indigenous peoples and the government is not about undermining responsible government; that is, the governor general's presence does not undermine the authority of Parliament. The Aboriginal peoples' desire for that presence simply means they want to ensure that the conversation goes beyond raw power – a context in which they have been continually betrayed. They want the conversation to include the ethical authority of the state, the Honour of the Crown. In other words, they believe that the presence of the governor general will invoke the centrality of the state's commitments made through the treaties. These treaties were signed not by the government but by the Crown, and therefore by the state, in the name of the people. And while our obligations are legal, they are first of all ethical.

This may seem, at first reading, a bit abstract or theoretical. After all, the governor general would not interfere in such a negotiation. Does that not mean his would be merely a ceremonial presence? And here you come up, once again, against the basic decline in how we tend to imagine governance. It must be *real* power or it is *mere* ceremony. The question is quite different when you alter the phrase to *real power* and *real authority*, and still more different when you understand that the point of authority is not interference. The governor general's presence, many Aboriginals feel, would impose a certain respect due to the senior elder in the land. And that should be a guarantee of the Crown acting with honour.

You may think this is a long shot. But either you believe in the legitimacy of the structures of the state or you don't. If you don't, then that leaves only power, which is a form of absolutism.

The experience of Aboriginal peoples over the last hundred and fifty years has come down to working with governments – and in particular the Department of Indian Affairs, itself arm in arm with the Ministry of Justice – that use their power to betray the Crown's obligations to respect and fulfill the treaties. Governments, one after the other, have acted as if they have the power to do whatever they want when it comes to indigenous peoples. As if they do not believe in the legitimacy of the structures of the state.

Here it is worth repeating the headlines: Residential schools. Limitations on religious freedom through the banning of ceremonies, of potlatches, of the right of spiritual leaders to travel. The bogus rule claiming that First Nations people needed permission to travel. Banning First Nations people from using lawyers. The underfunding of Aboriginal education. Interference in the use of their land. The steady removal of land by a variety of dubious methods. Etc. Etc. Etc.

In other words, governments, one after the other, have used their power to betray the Honour of the Crown.

That is why the Supreme Court in the Guerin case rebuked the federal government's misuse of its power. On the surface it was a mundane case of local Indian Affairs officers using their power to cheat the Musqueam Band out of money for land leased to rich Vancouverites to build a golf course. The Musqueam live on the south side of the city, and the Shaughnessy Heights Golf Club is still there. Over the decades, how many times in how many places has something like this happened? Thomas King presents an accurate and depressing account of this history of land pilfering in his *The Inconvenient Indian*. In the Musqueam case, the local officials and their friends in the city did their deal within their technical rights. However, knowing themselves that it was unethical, the officials refused to share documents with the band. Chief Guerin persisted in a saga that nine years later ended up at the Supreme Court.

But the Court chose not to base its ruling on such utilitarian concepts as the efficient use or the legal use of bureaucratic power. It did not focus in on the reform of the Department of Indian Affairs. All of these can be seen as required outcomes of the ruling. But the core of the Court's message was that the Government of Canada, in all its actions, was bound to respect ethical principles. These can be seen in two parts. First, Canada has a fiduciary duty or obligation to act in the best interests of Aboriginal people. This simple principle made Guerin one of the most important court cases of the twentieth century. Why? Because it took us back to the original principles of the Aboriginal–non-Aboriginal relationship. That relationship was developed in good faith, and therefore carried very real obligations. In the case of the Musqueam, the Crown had betrayed its obligations. And this led to the second, more basic understanding, which is now often seen as the broader outcome of Guerin. What is the basis of the fiduciary relationship? What is Canada's obligation? It is contained in the Honour of the Crown. From that core, the rest would follow. And this concept is so solid that more Aboriginals are now using it in cases against the government. As they should. This reality of the Honour of the Crown is an important Aboriginal contribution to justice for all Canadians. In fact, I believe that non-Aboriginals could use it in many government-related cases.

Chief Delbert Guerin, who led this long and difficult fight, died in May 2014. He was one of the great figures of contemporary Canada. By formally reintroducing ethics into the core of public administration, he changed the way we must think of ourselves. We owe him a great deal.

In the more than decade-long Delgamuukw case, the Supreme Court tied its ruling to the trustworthiness of the First Nations' oral interpretation of their rights rather than to the written version of officials. Again, there was a built-in assumption about the obligation of the Crown to act with honour.

There is a moving similarity in these cases, cases that are changing the nature of Canada. Delgamuukw involved two bands of the Skeena region in northwest British Columbia. They wanted to challenge the governmental and legal assumptions about land ownership. The case began in 1984 and ended at the Supreme Court in 1997. The two bands did not win ownership. However, they brought the standard European-derived assumptions about the nature of ownership to a halt and opened the way for what might be fair negotiations.

What is fascinating is that the government had all the written documentation it needed to win. But the court, led by Chief Justice Antonio Lamer, turned them back.

The Gitxsan and the Wet'suwet'en Nations had put forward an argument of oral memory in order to prove the land was theirs. They argued that oral memory is perfectly accurate, as it is passed on from one generation to the next via individuals charged with remembering, and with doing so accurately through a formalized process.

As in the Guerin decision, the Court chose to base its decision on principles far more important than any technical argument coming out of the Western tradition. The result was one of the most important rulings in the history of Canada. Alongside written proof, the Court would give equal place – and in this case what amounted to precedence – to oral memory. This argument for orality carries all of us out of the universal European narrative.

In the chief justice's eloquent judgment, he said that oral histories would be "admitted for their truth," that the laws of evidence must therefore be adapted, that "in the circumstances, the factual findings [of the government] cannot stand."

His concluding sentences were a call for negotiations to achieve something that I can only imagine happening through a spatial approach: "... the reconciliation of the pre-existence of Aboriginal societies with the sovereignty of the Crown. Let us face it, we are all here to stay."

The crisis of 2012–2013 is a depressing reminder that the governments of Canada – federal and provincial – have stubbornly refused to accept this Supreme Court recommendation. But at least the rules are there, carefully argued and laid out, constantly repeated and developed in case after case.

Guerin and Delgamuukw are two examples of the continuing ability of Aboriginal peoples to shape not just how Canada functions or will function, but how Canada imagines itself. The Court's decisions demonstrate how Canada does not exist or function merely in the narrative of the British or French philosophy of governance. It is beside the point that our governments at all levels, along with the legal profession, are trying to pretend that these rulings do not exist. Sooner or later they will have to accept that the Supreme Court exists and has ruled. More important, these arguments make sense, here.

Let me put this another way. Each time the Supreme Court rules on an Aboriginal question, it seems to feel obliged to engage in original thinking. Why? Because it comes up against the originality of the Canadian reality, in which indigenous ways of thinking can be as important as the imported European methods. Or more important.

There is another reason why the Court is forced onto the grounds of originality and principle. For almost a hundred and fifty years, politicians and civil servants have repeatedly acted as if there were no principles at stake. As if there were no intentional relationship, carefully worked out in treaties agreed to by both parties. There was only power. And they could use that power to serve narrow interests.

Does this mean that today there are no good people working in the Department of Indian Affairs? Not at all. What it does mean is that this department, whatever its current name, has neither ethical nor moral credibility. And I doubt that it can be reformed in order to assume the necessary ethical and moral credibility. The department has had a reasonable number of very good ministers who have attempted to change the situation. None has succeeded.

————

Allow me to tell you a short story about a long saga, both of which illustrate what the government has been doing and what the indigenous peoples have been dealing with over approximately a century and a half.

St. Anne's in Fort Albany on James Bay was opened in 1902 as a Roman Catholic mission. In 1904 it became a residential school. In 1970 the federal government took it over, closing it in 1976.

In the early 1990s, after widespread complaints of sexual and physical abuse against the children, Ontario Provincial Police detectives were assigned to investigate what had happened at the school. The result was several convictions. These came out of the massive investigations lasting five years and involving hundreds of survivors. Seven thousand pages of testimony and corroborated information were assembled. For example, there was an electric chair. Edmund Metatawabin, chief of the Fort Albany First Nation in the 1990s: "Small boys used to have their legs flying in front of them … the sight of a child being electrocuted and their legs flying out in front was a funny sight for the missionaries and they'd all be laughing … the cranking of the machine would be longer and harder. Now you're inflicted with real pain. Some of them passed out."

In 2003 the federal government asked for and received copies of these seven thousand pages.

Meanwhile the country was slowly developing a method aimed at reconciliation. It was formalized as the Indian Residential Schools Settlement Process. Victims were to register and then take part in a proceeding that was to be non-adversarial. It was, after all, supposed to be a healing process. The method was simple.

Our government – that is to say, you and I – admitted that wrongs had been committed. Victims were then to be listened to. Government and the churches were then to make a clean breast of what they had done. We know that this revelation/listening stage is a central part of any reconciliation process. It goes without saying that the government was expected to act honestly, to produce all information in its hands.

Instead, our government withheld a great deal of essential information. There were, they said, "no known documents of sexual abuse at Fort Albany Indian Residential School. No known incident documents of sexual abuse at Fort Albany IRS." This was a straight lie. Not only did they ignore a basic rule of our legal system – the duty to disclose – they ignored the specific requirements laid out in documents explaining the government's responsibilities in this reconciliation process.

What's more, they used the resulting lack of documented

information to throw into doubt, in an adversarial manner, the victims' stories. They converted a reconciliation process into an attempt to re-wound the wounded. They set out to humiliate the victims.

However, there was some knowledge that documents existed. The survivors asked for them and were rebuffed. Eventually they went to the courts and fought our government. In January 2014 the Ontario Superior Court forced our government to release the documents and so reveal that we – it is, after all, our government – had lied.

Justice Perell wrote that the government's refusal to admit to the contents of the seven thousand pages or to release them "had compromised the process and denied the claimants' access to justice." He wrote of governmental non-compliance.

In a pitiful misrepresentation of reality, an individual was made to say, on behalf of Aboriginal Affairs Minister Bernard Valcourt, "We are pleased the court clarified we can disclose the documents." Add to this an astonishing exchange of letters between the minister of justice, Peter MacKay, and an MP, Charlie Angus, and you begin to realize that our governmental attitudes have not fundamentally changed. Angus carefully points out the ministry's improper behaviour and misleading activities. The minister replies as if nothing is wrong and avoids mentioning or dealing with the two central issues: for eleven years the government had had the information necessary for a fair process and intentionally hidden that fact or pretended they could not release it; the government's lawyers had used this non-disclosure to undermine the First Nations victims. There is no suggestion from the minister of error. No contrition. No apology. Just a cold assertion that the department was doing its job.

In circumstances such as this I have no sympathy for myself as a citizen. It is my government, my civil service. Mine and yours. It has shamed all of us by prevaricating, lying, causing suffering to fellow citizens. In this case, the word *shame* must be used. We and those suffering are the Crown. We are the source of Canada's fiduciary responsibility. And we, through our government, are cheating and humiliating citizens who have already been humiliated by our governmental education system.

Not surprisingly, the survivors wrote to the minister of justice asking that he withdraw the department's lawyers from the process; they, the survivors, had "completely lost faith and trust" in them. "These lawyers, who are supposed to uphold the laws of Canada for all Canadians (including Aboriginal Canadians), have proved to be untruthful and unreliable."

---

This is just one story. How many others are there?

Note the similarity to the Guerin case: members of the Department of Indian Affairs use their administrative power to mislead Aboriginal people. They betray the Honour of the Crown.

This is one of the reasons that the then national chief, Shawn A-in-chut Atleo, insisted during the winter of 2012–2013 on a direct working relationship with the prime minister and the Privy Council. He knew that the First Nations must deal at that level because they are treaty partners, not wards of the state under the tutelage of a department. But he also knew that First Nations people must operate well above the corrupted systems of the Department of Indian Affairs as well as of Justice, systems originally created to destroy the department's "wards" or, as they now put it, "clients." The application of this commercial term to describe the relationship of citizens to the government they chose is both stupid and ignorant. The application of this term to indigenous peoples – treaty people – is, in addition, insulting. After all, what is a *client?* Someone who is buying goods or services based on the narrow self-interest of the seller on the one hand and of the buyer on the other. And so even this terminology is a constant reminder that Aboriginal peoples must rise above the paternalistic misuse of power on which the department has been built. They must negotiate at a higher level, as equals.

# V

# THE VICTORIAN
# POORHOUSE DEPARTMENT

All of this leads to a broader philosophical question. Once you separate authority and power, you are free to examine how the government understands this relationship versus how Aboriginals understand it.

In the second half of the nineteenth century, our government began to see treaties as classic commercial mechanisms for buying and selling land. What about their treaty obligations to the "Indians"? Well, the politicians and civil servants were part of the ethos of that time – an era of superior white men running empires for everyone else's own good. On the subject of Indians they did not even try to rise above the prejudices of the day. They were also working with the social mechanisms of the time – an era of poorhouses and indentured children. Remember the Irish famine that brought tens of thousands of powerless, destitute, starving, diseased, often dying people to Canada in the late 1840s? After having crossed the Atlantic in slave-like conditions they were left to die in large numbers on Grosse Isle near Quebec City. Most survivors were shipped on to Toronto in even worse conditions than those of the Atlantic crossing – the result of a corrupt Family Compact transport contract. In the summer of 1847, as the often contagious refugees tripled Toronto's population, the city faced a mortal crisis. The Family Compact's unwillingness to deal with the situation they had created led in good part to their first clear defeat in Upper Canada in the election of January 1848. And that in turn brought the Reformers to power under the leadership of Louis-Hippolyte LaFontaine and Robert Baldwin. The result was a multitude of serious reforms, beginning with Canada's first immigration policy law. But that was a short moment in a vast imperial era. Governments would go on struggling with the empire ethos for a long time. It was a terrible struggle, all around the world, in which mythologies of racial superiority, cultural loyalty to that race and class-based rights were used in a heavy-handed way to oppose local reforms, local justice and local responsibility.

In contradiction to these big political battles at the national level in Canada, a great deal was happening on the ground. Many new, cooperative approaches were emerging. A good part of this was somehow a continuation of the old indigenous influences and of the old indigenous–settler cooperative approaches. These mixed in with other influences, for example from the many small religious sects that were organized around cooperative principles. The overall outcome was a series of reform battles that led the federal government in particular to develop new social policies.

But Indian Affairs seemed to inherit the worst of the Victorian ethos – one filled with poorhouses and the wretched poor, an ethos based on charity and punishment, not justice. It was a paternalistic view of government. The egalitarianism and inclusiveness of Canadian social reforms owed part of their profound conceptualization to the long-standing partnership with Aboriginal peoples. Yet the Aboriginals themselves were increasingly left out of the programs, and out of the history of the creation of the programs.

So if you try to understand what went wrong in government relations with indigenous peoples, you can trace it in part to this Victorian poorhouse approach. Over the decades it evolved on the reserves into, at best, government housing for the poor, in which the poor are seen as passive people in need of control by others for their own good.

Whatever the department's policies today, they remain tainted by these fundamentally Victorian paternalistic assumptions. In other words, having in their minds bought the lands, governments continue to run them more or less as slum landlords. That the inhabitants have gradually gained back much of their original legal power – along with real political power, particularly since the last World War – has not changed the government's fundamental point of view. At best, the authorities are confused. How is it possible that passive people in need of control do not remain passive? And, among other things, how can it be possible that they regularly outsmart the government at the Supreme Court?

Am I exaggerating? If so, why is it that the government has always spent less on First Nations education than the provincial non-Aboriginal per capita rates? Why is there third-world water quality in so many communities? Why are the social facilities so poor on so many reserves? Why do almost half of Aboriginal children live in poverty? Why do the Indian Affairs and the Justice departments participate in a perpetual fight in the courts to oppose and limit land settlements?

The point is that there is no real administrative engagement with the indigenous reality. Is it surprising that the Department of Indian Affairs has no credibility among those citizens it exists to serve?

# VI

# THE RACIAL LENS

There is one other important, more profound way to see this situation. Look at our history. The structures within which Aboriginals must work have been artificially put in place by governments, largely by London and Ottawa, actively supported by provincial governments. British Columbia, with its determined blockage of treaty negotiations, deserves special mention. And what are these structures? *Treaty versus non-Treaty Indians. Status versus non-Status Indians. Status* or *non-Status* based on what are effectively complex calculations of blood.

Imagine! We have imposed on Aboriginal people a method of calculation that defines their rights and place in society. And that calculation is based on the worst form of European racism, which assumes there is virtue in the purity of blood lineage. This method was formalized in the second half of the nineteenth century, when the empires were busy justifying their growing power on the basis of Darwinian racial superiority. This required a measurement of race. Blood was a pseudo-scientific characteristic useful in the creation of a racial pecking order. And it could be applied to all peoples with the certainty that science – being European – would put the Europeans on top. What was absolutely clear in this

Darwinesque theory was that interracial marriages produced a dilution of blood. A watering down of purity, and therefore of such things as nobility of character and intelligence. How fortunate that modern science could be invoked in support of the British, French, German, American and Italian empires. Better still, progress and a racial pecking order and blood purity could be linked. Imperial officials, succeeded by Canadian officials, could apply all this to the administration of Indian affairs. Science comforting power! A wonderful coincidence. No! No! There is no lucky accident here. It is destiny. Wonderful, disinterested, Darwinian destiny.

But it doesn't stop there. This is grand theory. Global. All-inclusive. It encompasses the natural superiority of men over women. Long after 1982, when equal rights for women were given constitutional status in the Charter of Rights and specifically for Aboriginal women in the amended constitution itself, the patriarchal truth of the Indian Act is still being picked away at. The status of men versus the status of women is only one part of this. Rights on- versus off-reserve. Marrying non-Aboriginals and losing status because of watered-down blood. And on and on.

All of this was invented by imperial-minded officials who saw the world through a racial lens. They brought with them from Britain their racial views and legally enveloped the whole Aboriginal world within them. These views were taken up by the Department of Indian Affairs and those who worked in this domain. All of us were partly trapped by such delusional European beliefs in the centrality of race. Today it is fairly safe to say that most Canadians have escaped from it. But the assumptions of the late-nineteenth-century legal system leave Aboriginals largely trapped within its logic. And imperial systems are always designed to divide those who are to be dominated. It is easier to dominate people if you can divide them against each other. Race, religion, territory and the assignment of privileges are the traditional tools.

Again, these racial theories are not Aboriginal concepts. Again, this is a case where blame needs to be assigned. Again, this humiliating and divisive system was not of their doing.

# VII

# FORMS OF ARGUMENT

One of the outcomes of the European racial lens is that the richness of opinions in the indigenous world is reduced to a situation of either/or, unity versus division, exclusion versus inclusion. The fluidity of complex traditional systems is broken down into particles of formal democracy so that First Nations people cannot easily use the elected-chief system. It encourages an adversarial approach in small communities, where it is divisive and destructive, with winners and losers, while undermining a more appropriate search for consensus. And it does not deal with the reality of half the Aboriginal population living off-reserve, in cities where they are creating an interesting new Aboriginal phenomenon as well as an interesting new urban phenomenon.

Having imposed an inappropriate system, the Department of Indian Affairs and their lawyers seem to take pleasure in either standing back waiting for a disaster or intervening in a heavy-handed, paternalistic way. The First Nations Transparency law, enacted in 2014, is a perfect example. The department has had more than a half century to work carefully with the reserves on financial systems, to help through training, on-the-ground support and the advice of accountants. They failed in this most basic service. In 2005, a large program called Accountability for Results was put in place by the AFN, the auditor general and the Treasury Board. These three were to cooperate in establishing transparency in the Department of Indian Affairs and on the reserves. Everyone, except perhaps the Department, wanted to know what was happening to the money. Today the Department receives some 8 billion dollars annually, and there is no public sense of how it spends this money. In 2014, acting National Chief Ghislain Picard called it "a bloated, inefficient and

Hayden King, Anishinaabe, one of the new voices of Aboriginal leadership. A professor and director of Indigenous Governance at Ryerson University. © *Windspeaker*/AMMSA.

unaccountable bureaucracy." When the Conservative government came to power it shut down this program, which was aimed in good part at departmental transparency. Now, with the Transparency Act, the government has set out to reveal wrongdoing by chiefs, not the Department. There is nothing wrong with the act except the context, the attitude and the political purpose.

Sure enough a few delinquent chiefs have been uncovered. The media then focused on them, as if they were representative of all chiefs. But the reality is that very few chiefs were found to be acting badly. Most were found to be underpaid.

Did anyone bother to compare the percentage of overpaid chiefs with the percentage of overpaid CEOs in the private sector? The percentage of corrupt or incompetent chiefs with the percentage of corrupt or incompetent mayors? Toronto, Montreal, Laval and London come to mind, representing a large percentage of Canada's population. On August 2, 2014, Hayden King published a fine analysis of the Transparency Act.

Quite simply, the Ottawa-imposed old imperial model does not help. Indigenous leaders must spend much of their time struggling with how to handle it. At some point the Indian Act system will go. But that will be the result of a broad conversation involving Aboriginals and non-Aboriginals over how to settle the outstanding treaty, land and other issues. This won't necessarily require a protracted debate. What it will require is that Canadians engage in the conversation instead of sitting back as if it doesn't concern them. We have to be involved because what is needed is a serious transfer of responsibility and money, the exact opposite of dragging out treaty negotiations one by one. We need to do more than empower our governments to act. We need to push them. We need to make this a make-or-break issue. We need to elect or defeat them with these indigenous issues in mind.

We have become used to the absence of real public debate on almost any topic. Instead, every day, we are presented with predigested packages of what must be done. These packages often come in statements or speeches presented by ministers who have hardly read them in advance. Or they have talking points and stick to them. Or there is the technocratic-populist model in which a utilitarian proposal is made, followed by a tear-jerker story – *Last week in (small town), Mary Smith told me....* Or we are induced to focus on a particular financial or administrative detail by the opposition parties and press: someone has lied and must be punished; someone has cheated and must be broken. These transgressions are then flogged until someone's career dies. Fine. There may indeed have been corruption or laziness or whatever. And punishment is appropriate. And it may signal something larger – for example, that a government has passed its best-before date. But none of this constitutes the public debate that makes democracy work. It is rhetoric. And this *off with his head* procedure produces the sort of public argument that brings any discussion about ideas to an end. Or it is an expansion of populism, as in: drag down the rich and powerful. Except this method is an illusion. One or two villains fall, and their destruction protects the system and the others. Not only is this not an expression of democracy, it is exactly the system traditionally used by absolute monarchs to divert criticism from themselves. There is, for example, no fundamental tax reform, no breaking up of monopolies.

And so we are not at all prepared for the spilling out of real debate – unruly, not prepackaged, containing natural contradictions. We are even less prepared, for example, for First Nations' approaches to debate. This might involve an interesting use of memory, a broader sense of history, a non-power-based approach to relationships. Much of this has a circular feel to it, quite different from the dominant linear, managerial, utilitarian language we have become used to. It has nothing to do with the old scapegoat system, in which the king, in order to clear the air, satisfies the public's hunger for a sacrificial victim.

There is a certain style to Aboriginal debates that is not European-derived. It may include elements of the European tradition and it may be coming from people with PhDs or MAs, but there is a complexity to it that does not fit, for example, with the idea of a solitary heroic leader/speaker/image bearer, the prime minister or president who is the leader. *She who must be obeyed,* as they used to say of Mrs. Thatcher. This obsession with The Leader, with power, alongside the absence of internal debate is such a curious concept to have arisen in democracies. And I am not simply referring to the obsession of political operators and commentators with image and control – the leader's image, the control over debate and policy. What we are dealing with is an approach to leadership whose modern origins lie in Bonaparte, in his Napoleonic focus on the image of the Heroic Leader, thanks to which he could exercise far more power than is intended in the democratic system. Yet this is the approach to leadership sought by political organizers throughout the Western democracies.

Historically, each First Nation had three or four leaders – the hereditary chief, the fire keeper or spiritual leader, the military leader and what we would today call the elected chief. Big Bear and Poundmaker were chosen chiefs – more or less elected – in the second half of the nineteenth century. They

Pitikwahanapiwiyin "Poundmaker" (1842–1886), Plains Cree. One of the
great chiefs of the Prairies in the second half of the nineteenth century.
A sophisticated peacemaker destroyed by the events of 1885. Note the chain
leading to an ankle iron. Somehow in this photograph he rises above the
humiliation of his arrest and trial. © Library and Archives Canada, C001875.

were chosen for their ability to lead and to hold together societies in which full, open, fundamentally oral argument was much admired. These debates would include other elders with opinions and different, sometimes critical roles for women. Amidst all of that the chosen leader would need to carry the broad argument over the long rough-and-tumble debates that led to decisions.

And because these debates were about community, the community's relationship to place and the complex relationship between the various sorts of leaders and elders, they would rarely lead to a simple understanding of winners and losers.

That is part of the context for the rough-and-tumble of AFN politics. The press corps tends to see this only in their own terms – a Manichaean struggle ending with winners and losers. They don't understand or don't want to understand the powerful orality in these arguments, the absence of the prepackaged technocratic messages most of us are now addicted to, the complexity of the social structures involved.

Over the winter of 2012–2013 the parliamentary press corps reported endlessly on profound divisions in the First Nations community. It was these opposing positions that they focused on, and so we, the reading public, could not help but be riveted by the actions of one chief or another. Would Chief Spence break her fast? Would one or another go to a meeting with the prime minister? Would the presence of the governor general change this? These were presented as clear and irreconcilable divisions. Make-or-break gestures. Make-or-break meetings.

Except that the next day that same chief would make little of it, mentioning that he had decided to go or not to go to the meeting in question on the basis of a particular sense of obligation. And that was all. There was no irreconcilable division; in the long run, there was hardly any difference of opinion. The press were confused, and concluded that the chief in question had backed down. It scarcely occurred to them to try to understand the nature of the debate going on.

Does that mean there are no divisions? No. Of course there are differences of opinion. Are they important? Perhaps. Perhaps not. But many things are happening on many levels. And to the extent that any divisions are real they are in good part an outcome of the old imperially imposed system of governance. Even if a few words have been changed, the Indian Act still functions as if First Nations peoples are wards of the state. The elected chiefs must manoeuvre around this. Young people quite naturally do not feel part of it. Why should they?

And here is the essential point. Aboriginal peoples have a hundred and fifty years of experience with Ottawa's attempting to impose its idea of argument, of concluding that First Nations debate should be taken at European-style face value. This has been used to impose the methods of written law. And to use First Nations debates in order to divide them. In this way Canadian authorities managed to win many legal and administrative battles in the first half of the twentieth century.

What has changed on that front is the clarity coming out of the courts, and the Supreme Court in particular, which has meant a gradual rolling-back of those government victories that were based on a linear, utilitarian, heavily written approach to the law. Instead, in such cases as Delgamuukw, Sparrow and Haida, they have recognized elements of oral memory based not on the letter of the law but on the intent of the original agreements. They have answered questions centred on ethics.

They have attempted to understand circular concepts as well as indigenous beliefs about relationships, both among people and between people and place. The Court has not ordered governments to comply. But it has made it clear that

Niigaan Sinclair, Anishinaabe, professor, activist, writer, editor. An important voice in the new leadership. © Niigaanwewidam Sinclair.

governments must take these more inclusive interpretations into account.

The result is that Aboriginal peoples can now engage in broad public arguments built within a different framework. They can assert with confidence that the Canadian authorities have not been listening, that they have not even tried to understand the real meaning of what their interlocutors were saying. Worse still, it is clear that our governments have been intentionally trying to impose narrow, self-serving interpretations on whatever they hear. And have done so since the second half of the nineteenth century.

Aboriginal leaders have gradually worked out how to deal with these interlocutors. When I talk of a tough, sophisticated new elite, I am talking about people who can see these tactics coming a long way off. Their many victories at the Supreme Court are a sign that the lesson has been learned by at least some parts of the Canadian system of governance. To this we must add the admirable flexibility in Aboriginal strategies that allows them to avoid many of the utilitarian and Manichaean traps set for them by Canadian authorities and by many Canadian journalists.

———

The truth is that most Canadians seem weary of the old politics practised by our federal and provincial authorities. Most seem to want to move on, if only they could work out how.

Of course a few haven't moved at all. Some with influence still believe in the old assimilation arguments. They have not evolved beyond the Trudeau White Paper of 1969, which was the last broadly articulated attempt at assimilation. In the name of European-style nationalism and Darwinian determinism, this small group holds on to the old concepts of superiority, which they continually reintroduce, with little refinements, as inevitable and modern.

But Trudeau himself quickly moved beyond his own initiative. He began to include indigenous leaders to some extent in federal–provincial meetings. He oversaw a revamped Constitution in which Aboriginal rights were recognized. Turner, Mulroney, Chrétien and Martin: each prime minister contributed new bits and pieces, even if none did what was necessary. Turner, as justice minister, introduced some Aboriginal legal concepts into the court system. Martin began a serious reform – the Kelowna Accord – but did not survive in office to put it in place.

I am convinced that all four knew there was no turning back. Perhaps none had fully focused on the indigenous comeback and its full implications. But they knew the situation had changed.

Mr. Harper made a full apology, in 2008, for the residential schools. He must surely sense the breadth of the changes under way and the looming dangers, which are enormous. As are the opportunities. He hates to fail, and history has handed him a central role at a historic moment in this Canadian drama. A prime minister has the responsibility and the opportunity to help us back onto an honest track. By strengthening our foundations, of which treaties are a central part, our present reality will be strengthened in turn.

# VIII

# FAMILY NAMES

The First Nations see the treaties very clearly, and, again, the Supreme Court has repeatedly made it plain over the last few decades that the Aboriginals are right, the government wrong.

Right about what?

That the crude European concept of ownership – a great deal of control with very little responsibility – has been artificially imposed on the situation. That people belong to families and communities, which are part of a territory. The point is not one of ownership of land; they have responsibility within it, not over it.

Through the treaties, non–First Nations people entered into various First Nations circles. We became part of those families and communities. Authorities like the governor general were called "grandfather," Queen Victoria "grandmother," and the prime minister "father," not because the "Indians" were children – as London and Ottawa chose to interpret these words – but because such people were treated as elders in the family. They deserved terms of respect along with other elders. Governor General Lorne was called "brother-in-law" because he had married Queen Victoria's daughter. Great, much-admired chiefs or fire keepers were often called grandfathers; at a lesser level they were fathers. And if people of power meet to discuss arrangements, well, the elders must be present to represent the unwritten authority of the community.

In this context, the treaty people, all of us, are bound by our shared obligations as family and community members, whether we are elders or active adults or children. Our responsibilities are tied not to power relationships, but rather to the obligations of shared belonging.

This is a sophisticated and accurate representation of our reality. And we are particularly lucky because this interpretation represents a powerful tool for the way most Canadians imagine their country.

# IX

# COMING BACK

Let me go back to what most non-Aboriginal Canadians think of as the central Aboriginal problems. These could be summarized as problems of family and social breakdown.

First, it is important to assign blame. This is not always so – often it is best to let bygones be bygones. But in this case, long-term responsibility shapes what can and should happen now. We have to know what has been done, who did it and whether they had some level of permission to do what they did. Our society needs to understand all of this in order to assume responsibility in a real way, and then to act differently. That process will shape who First Nations peoples are willing to trust, negotiate with and work with.

The reality is that the social, family and political problems we are so focused on are almost entirely, directly or indirectly, the outcome of the long-term behaviour of federal and provincial governments. And that behaviour is the outcome of socially accepted attitudes in the citizenry.

Think of the revelation in July 2013 that malnourished First Nations children had been used as guinea pigs in health tests. Think of the ongoing refusal of governments to face up to the implications of the murder and disappearance of indigenous women. Who is being protected? Police forces?

Local elites? The reputation of communities? The image that we as Canadians wish to have of ourselves? That we wish to project to others?

The private sector has also, and often, been an offending party. But that is largely because laws or regulations made it possible, or because police or public administrators collaborated in making the wrongdoing possible. Were they corrupted? Complicit? A simple example of this was the improper removal of Musqueam land facilitated by public officials in order to allow Vancouverites to build the Shaughnessy Heights Golf Club.

If First Nations insist so much on upholding treaties, it is in good part because one of the two signatories – us – has consistently and consciously broken the agreements.

Of course, this doesn't free Aboriginals of responsibility for their actions. Nor for the most part do they seek to avoid responsibility. But the past does shape what most individuals feel they can do today. This is hardly a controversial idea.

So, I repeat, the blame must be clearly assigned and assumed by Canadian society and its governing institutions.

———

Second, and curiously enough more important, Aboriginals do not see their difficulties as the central issue. They do not see themselves in the negative terms that give such guilt-ridden comfort to many Canadians. As I have already said, I don't hear them asking to be locked into the category of victim. In spite of their difficulties, the overriding atmosphere among First Nations, Métis and Inuit is one of optimism. They are conscious of how hard they have had to fight over the last century, first to survive as people and cultures and second to rebuild their position.

Think about their efforts.

The highest per capita enlistment in the two World Wars – a statement of self-confidence. Endless letters, petitions, protests, provocations, demonstrations, refusals. The 1910 letter presented by the British Columbia chiefs to Wilfrid Laurier is just one example among thousands. And then there are all those court cases, one after the other, dragging on for years, usually lost in the lower courts then fought through to

Edmond Gagne (1921– ), Métis, standing at the rear left of his landing craft, going in on D-Day. He was badly wounded one month later. Gagne was in D Company, The Winnipeg Rifles. C Company, including a number of other indigenous soldiers and my father, Bill Saul, was on another landing craft not far away. © Canada Dept. of National Defence/Library and Archives Canada/PA-132651.

the Supreme Court. Two Royal Commissions. The first, from 1974 to 1977, was supposed to be about a pipeline. After all, it was called the Mackenzie Valley Pipeline Inquiry. It wasn't supposed to be a four-year inquisition of established government/industry practices and one of the launch pads for the new indigenous movement. But its head, Justice Thomas Berger, came to understand that his role was to open up a space for the new generation of Aboriginal leaders and their advisers. Hence the title of the final report: *Northern Frontier, Northern Homeland*.

Then came the Erasmus–Dussault Royal Commission, led by the former national chief, Georges Erasmus, and Justice René Dussault. Successive governments have tried to ignore it. But its 1996 report is a remarkable combination of research and analysis. In its four thousand pages, the true nature of the Aboriginal role in Canada is fully uncovered and reasserted. Its recommendations are of enormous importance. But the research it represented, along with the resulting volumes of historic texts, alone made the commission invaluable. A hundred and forty years of denial, prevarication, misrepresentation and simple historical rewriting by government after government, historian after historian, interest group after interest group, had been swept away. These two inquiry commissions put in place the intellectual, social and political basis for today's wave of indigenous revival.

And then, of course, there are the treaty negotiations and renegotiations, intentionally dragged out by our governments. As I said earlier, the Nisga'a negotiation alone went on for twenty-five years, wasting Nisga'a and taxpayer money, eating up the lives of a whole generation. But they persisted.

Yes, what we are witnessing is a continuing and strengthening comeback.

And, yes, non-Aboriginals have a choice. We can go on allowing our governments and power systems and corporations to slow or attempt to stop or deform this return of the founding peoples to their proper place. Or we can learn to listen and to understand what is happening. And then we can ensure that we do not continue to be the problem.

Let me put this another way. I believe that whatever governments in Canada do, positive or negative, indigenous peoples will continue to grow in strength and influence. The question that each of us must ask ourselves is whether we want to play our role as citizens – as treaty people. Or whether we are going to hang on to our old habits – no matter how disguised as sympathy or ignorance or technical difficulties or legal difficulties or budgetary difficulties – and so betray our obligations as Canadian citizens.

# X

# A NEW ELITE

What does this comeback look like?

First, there is the simple matter of size. Over four centuries ago as many as two million First Nations people took in small groups of lost and confused Europeans. Joseph Boyden gives you a good sense of that atmosphere in his novel *The Orenda*. It would be a good two hundred and fifty years before the newcomers reached the population numbers of the Aboriginals and began to know their way around. For two and a half to three and a half centuries – depending on where you were in Canada – Aboriginals maintained their numbers and continued to lead or to be active partners. Most Canadians know the names of a few great Aboriginal leaders – Joseph Brant; Tecumseh; John Norton, who led the Six Nations force at Queenston Heights and turned the battle against the Americans; Cuthbert Grant, captain-general of the Métis. In the last few years before the precipitous decline: Gabriel Dumont, Big Bear, Louis Riel, Crowfoot, Poundmaker. And then there are some who are known by small groups. A single example: Charles Edenshaw, the great Haida artist and hereditary chief of the late nineteenth century. But there were hundreds and hundreds of other important figures whose

Thayendanegea "Joseph Brant" (1743–1807), Mohawk. Linguist, great war leader, statesman, writer, founder of the Six Nations settlement on the Grand River in southern Ontario. Painted here by Gilbert Stuart (1755–1828) in 1786. Oil on canvas, H 30" x W 25", N0199.1961. Gift of Stephen C. Clark, Fenimore Art Museum, Cooperstown, New York. Photograph by Richard Walker.

names were excluded from the European-oriented history and mythology of Canada.

The point is that for centuries the Aboriginals showed enormous generosity and welcomed the newcomers into their circles. Then, under great stress, their population plummeted. Now, in just a century, that population has exploded up to well over a million. With the highest growth rates in Canada, Aboriginals are well on their way back to numbering two million and more.

This may well present an administrative challenge for all governments. They moan about how difficult it is to serve people living in the north, living in small, isolated communities. But don't we want Canadians living throughout Canada? Is there a policy in place that says we should all live in cities in the south? Besides, I thought we wanted population growth. That's one of the reasons for our immigration policy. Why is this seen as a problem simply because it is happening with Aboriginals?

The answer is that it isn't a problem. It is an opportunity. When you think how much was done to encourage the disappearance of these peoples, it is actually a civilizational triumph.

Two million may not at first seem enormous in a population of thirty-four million. But Aboriginal peoples are now one of the largest cultural groups in the country. Combine that size with their historic role, their treaty powers, their legal and constitutional positions and their influence over large stretches of commodity-rich land. Think of them as the majority, or the near majority, or the second-largest group in the three northern territories as well as in Labrador, the northern half of Quebec, Ontario, Manitoba, Saskatchewan, Alberta and British Columbia. Soon to be one-third of the Saskatchewan workforce. Think of them as the single most convincing argument for Canadian legitimacy in the Arctic. Think of their continuing victories in the courts, re-establishing the historic balance.

These numbers and legal strengths are now attached to an important factor of leadership. Today, at any one time, more than thirty thousand indigenous youth are enrolled in universities and colleges. This has been achieved in a half century. Yes, the percentages are below national averages. But the growth rate is well above. Graduates are pouring out.

This represents a remarkable new elite. Yes, elite. These are smart, tough, intellectually lean, rightfully angry young people. They remind me of the new Quebec elite of the 1960s. These graduates include professors, spread across the country. A handful I know or have met come to mind – Niigaan James Sinclair at the University of Manitoba, Hayden King at Ryerson University, Lorena Fontaine at the University of Winnipeg, Brock Pitawanakwat at the University of Sudbury, Michael Doxtater at McGill, Bob Watts at Queen's. So many of the new leaders are women, like the founders of Idle No More, Nina Wilson, Sylvia McAdam, Jessica Gordon and their non-Aboriginal friend Sheela McLean. Many are rising writers, fiction and non-fiction, like Leanne Simpson. There are engineers, doctors, nurses, teachers, consultants, administrators and, yes, politicians. In 2013, Michael DeGagné became the first indigenous intellectual to be named president of a Canadian chartered university – Nipissing in North Bay.

––––––

In the midst of this change there is a particularly moving phenomenon. For almost a century the destructive power of racism led many young Métis to melt into the population, rewarded for being white. These cannot have been easy choices, but they were the outcome of a concerted settler effort to demean the Métis people. Today the number of Métis is growing rapidly, in good part because young people – a new generation – are now assuming their origins.

This is not as easy as it sounds. They come from families who went through the painful process of redefining themselves in public as non-Aboriginal, often out of economic necessity. I have talked with some of these young people, often university students. They are at an age when choices all seem difficult or awkward. But these students are reimagining themselves completely, giving themselves new strength.

——

Think also of the great artists. Bill Reid, Alanis Obomsawin, Susan Point, Jim Hart, Georges Sioui, Robert Davidson, Tomson Highway, Jeannette Armstrong, Louise Halfe, Joseph Boyden, Kent Monkman, Thomas King, Richard Wagamese, Judas Ullulaq, Zacharia Kunuk, Kenojuak Ashevak, Gerald McMaster, Drew Hayden Taylor, Jane Ash Poitras, Norval Morrisseau and dozens of others. Think of new public figures like Wab Kinew or A Tribe Called Red.

In 1927 the government made it illegal for "Indians" to hire lawyers (Section 141 of the Indian Act). Today there are over one thousand Aboriginal lawyers and over thirty judges. Many of today's leading activists are women lawyers, like the Mi'Kmaq intellectual Pam Palmater and the remarkable Métis courtroom force Jean Teillet. Add to that the fascinating legal historians who lie behind many of the court challenges – Sakej Henderson is only one example. I should add here the growing number of philosophers putting forward different

A Tribe Called Red – Ian Campeau (Nipissing First Nation), Bear Thomas and Dan General (both Cayuga) – are champions of urban youth, blending powwow vocals, drumming and electronic music. Photo by Pat Balduc, courtesy of A Tribe Called Red.

versions of their non-linear, spatial or circular philosophies. Leroy Little Bear, Taiaiake Alfred, E. Richard Atleo (Umeek), to name only a few of the senior figures.

But why so many lawyers? Because governments and corporations used the law against indigenous people throughout the late nineteenth and twentieth centuries. The only way to fight back was to use that same legal system.

Many of these lawyers are very young. They will probably take on different roles, beyond mere law, from government to politics to business. This brings me back to the historic series of court victories that are changing Canada for the better, without most Canadians realizing it is happening, while our governments remain in denial.

From right to left: Melissa Daniels (Athabasca Chipewyan First Nation)
called to the Bar of Alberta by Provincial Court Judge Danielle Dalton
(Métis) and board member of the Canadian Association of Provincial Court
Judges, witnessed by her aunt Jude Daniels, a senior lawyer.
© *Alberta Sweetgrass*/AMMSA.

Why, for almost forty years now, have Aboriginal peoples
won virtually every time they go to the Supreme Court?
Because our history and the law, if fairly interpreted, cannot
help but re-establish our long-standing – long betrayed –
agreements. If I look for the leading constitutional voice of
historical accuracy and ethical understanding in Canada over
the last few decades, the sound is clear. It comes from the
indigenous community and the Supreme Court's rulings on
Aboriginal issues. Some people protest that this is judicial
interference in the political sphere. They are missing the point.
It is happening because the political class and the civil service
are not only not doing their job, they are acting badly. The
indigenous community, on the other hand, is paying attention

to our history and to our legal history. The Supreme Court is responding intelligently to this reality.

This doesn't explain why governments, the legal profession in general and much of the private sector have gone on acting as if Supreme Court decisions such as Delgamuukw, Guerin and the Haida case on consultation simply didn't happen. They are faced with compliance or denial. The fact is that these rulings and many more did happen. There have been several subsequent decisions repeating and reinforcing the government's obligation to consult. Eventually those with the power of government will be obliged to respect the law.

I have met throughout my life remarkable local Aboriginal leaders, among them Chief Guerin of the Musqueam; Chief Guujaaw of the Haida and Chief Gosnell of the Nisga'a; David Chartrand, president of the Manitoba Métis; Roberta Jamieson, former chief of the Six Nations; and Clifford Moar, former chief of the Mashteuiatsh First Nation.

Just think of the last few national chiefs: Georges Erasmus, Ovide Mercredi, Matthew Coon Come, Phil Fontaine, Shawn A-in-chut Atleo; or of Clément Chartier, president of the Métis National Council; or in the Arctic, Jose Kusugak, John Amagoalik, Mary Simon, Siila Watt-Cloutier, Jack Anawak, Paul Okalik, Eva Aariak. Behind these leaders is a large wave of new faces already in public life, one way or another. Again a handful of names come to mind: Clint Davis, who ran the Canadian Council for Aboriginal Business; J.P. Gladu, who runs it now; Wade Grant, a Musqueam councillor on the West Coast; Sandra Inutiq, the Nunavut language commissioner; Natan Obed, director of Nunavut Tunngavik; Kirt Ejesiak, who is on the executive council of the Inuit Circumpolar

Council; Mark Podlasly, founder of Brookmere Management Group; Madeleine Redfern, who has been mayor of Iqaluit and executive director of the Qikiqtani Truth Commission. Think of the remarkable figures who changed the history of northern Quebec: Billy Diamond, Ted Moses, Romeo Saganash.

And this is only a tiny sliver of the indigenous leadership, which demonstrates how complex and interesting their new elite is.

What is true is that they are faced with almost impossible political and social situations. But then they are the product of even more difficult situations. They are tough and highly conscious of the challenges.

# XI

# STUBBORN VINDICTIVE BABIES

In the midst of the dramatic events during the winter of 2012–2013, the Federal Court ruled that Métis and non–Status Indians had the same rights as Status Indians under the Constitution. This gives them access to First Nations programs and therefore would add hundreds of thousands of people to federal responsibilities. It was pure chance that this happened in the middle of the crisis. Yet it was also a sign of our evolution. And it was a reminder of the fundamental solidity of the Aboriginal position when it comes to justice – justice in the full sense. The simple truth is that cases will go on being won by those who seek to re-establish the agreements upon which Canada is built. In other words, in the midst of an emotional and complex national crisis, this court decision came as a clear sign of the direction our society is going. It would have been wise for those in power to embrace the outcome as a sign of understanding.

Instead we were treated to virtual silence, plus the standard reaction by the legal mainstream and commentators in the press. *This ruling was a problem. In difficult times too much money was involved. The ruling only stated a principle; surely it didn't need to be enforced. Perhaps it could be ignored.*

In other words, all the old habits of dry, hypocritical,

administrative and legal game playing by Canada's leadership in governments re-emerged. The mainstream interpreters of, and commentators on, public affairs trotted out their standard views. No one in power seems ready to acknowledge that injustice is resolved by justice.

Few commentators seem ready to re-examine their certitudes. Why not simply embrace the reality of the Aboriginal comeback? Why not accept that these court victories contain the elements for resolving the problem of Aboriginal poverty by creating the basis for Aboriginal power, which is in part economic power? We are dealing with a point-of-view problem. The Canadian government's point of view was set in the imperial/colonial era. Our dominant mythologies were shaped in the same era. All our governments – federal and provincial – must simply let go of their paternalistic mindset. Aboriginals are not wards of the state. They don't need charity. They want the power that our own history says is theirs by right. And that power contains economic solutions.

What this means is that our governments should stop wasting our money fighting to maintain systems of injustice. What they need to do is digest reality and embrace reconciliation, which, as Taiaiake Alfred says, begins with restitution. This is more than good intentions. It involves a shift in power and in economic wealth. That shift in economic wealth is the solution to Aboriginal poverty.

Unable to face this shift, our government is following the old strategy of playing for time. It is listening to the same old defensive, combative lawyers. And so they appealed the Federal Court decision on the status of Métis and non–Status Indians. Why? To humiliate a group of Canadians? To waste taxpayers' money? Because they could not bring themselves to think of Aboriginals in any real way as central to the living foundations of Canada? Or is it because they are simply unable to accept their responsibility as our representatives – as the representatives of the treaty people?

Gabriel Dumont (1837–1906), genius of guerrilla warfare, political and military leader in the fight for Métis rights. © Glenbow Museum, NA-1063-1.

Fifteen months later the Federal Court of Appeal ruled to sustain the Métis ruling while non-status cases would have to be dealt with case by case. No doubt some in Ottawa saw this as a partial victory. In reality, once you add up the case-by-case costs, the result will probably be far more expensive. Meanwhile, an opportunity to be positive and inclusive had been lost.

# XII

# POWER ON THE LAND

Despite governmental prevarication, these repeated legal victories and the progress – horribly slow but nevertheless progress – in treaty settlements are creating a new reality on the land.

There is an ironic, darkly comic side to the situation. In many treaty negotiations during the second half of the nineteenth century and early in the twentieth, government negotiators tried to push First Nations off arable lands and into the rock and forest. Immigrants wanted farmland. But today Canada is more dependent than it has been for half a century on commodities – mining, oil and gas, forestry. Where are these commodities? Largely in the rocks and forest.

Very present in these interior and northern regions – reinforced by numbers and the law – indigenous peoples are in an increasingly powerful and strategic position.

By the simple decision not to cooperate, they could bring the Canadian economy in good part to a halt. This is true. And this has been threatened by some. Ask yourself this question: What would you do if you had their experience of betrayal and denial and were now in their position? Is there any reason why they should stand by and allow the riches to flow south as they have for so long? They are increasingly in a strong position to get a fair share or to determine the shape of what happens or does not happen. Look at the pipeline debates of 2012–2014. The balance of power is changing. Once the First Nations in British Columbia made it clear that they would not go along with the Enbridge Northern Gateway pipeline, the B.C. government seemed to have few realistic choices. Besides, the idea of an Aboriginal–non-Aboriginal consensus has become important in B.C. And there is already a consensus between Aboriginals and the environmental movement. This slowly emerging reality is not the result of an abrupt change. You could see its early shapes in the hydro settlements of northern Quebec decades ago. The result there is that some of the largest corporations in the north

"There is already a consensus between Aboriginals and the environmental movement." © Zack Embree.

belong to Inuit and Cree. These are powerful and well-run operations. Makivik Corporation, in Nunavik in northern Quebec, for example, has used its role throughout the Arctic to ensure that there is decent transport through First Air.

Or go to the annual meeting of the Canadian Council for Aboriginal Business. You will see thousands of up-and-coming indigenous business leaders. Many of the big commodities companies have understood this. They are increasingly negotiating with indigenous peoples – in a new way – over participation, profit sharing, training, jobs. Not all of them, of course. As a First Nations engineer consultant friend of mine said, "A lot of them think if they delay long enough the world will go back to 1952." In Canada it will not, for all the reasons I have been explaining.

Of course, these are still early days. And this is a new type of relationship. After all, mining and forestry executives have a strong tradition of very narrow, very linear attitudes. Often that is helpful in this kind of business. Why? Because they are struggling more often than not against nature at its toughest. So they succeed because they themselves are tough and focused in a narrow way.

But the ability to build roads through wild mountains, to seek out minerals in isolated places, to tunnel into an unwilling earth, does not necessarily suggest a talent for human or societal relationships. Look around the world. Look over the last century and a half. Extraction industries have never been associated with democracy. It is a brutal, often violent history. Local inhabitants, Aboriginal or not, are in the way, unless they are on the payroll or can be bought off.

Fortunately a new generation of mining leaders is coming along, brought up in the era of environmentalism and indigenous rights. They know this is reality. How many there will be of this sort versus new generations of the old sort, we don't know.

Either way, they are businesspeople. The last thing they want is the forest roads or mine roads blocked by angry locals. If they are smart, they would rather negotiate than fight.

But the long-term key to such negotiations has four parts. First, it is true that indigenous people want more on-site jobs, the sort that are well paid, usually shorter term and hands on, such as working in the mine, cutting the trees, driving the trucks. Second, and more important at this stage, What about the indigenous managers, lawyers, accountants? They want their share of the longer-term top jobs, but these are rarely forthcoming because of the corporate mentality.

These first two elements are more complicated than they at first seem. The basic on-site jobs still require very specific training and experience. A young person in an isolated northern community is unlikely to have either. The traditional private-sector answer to this challenge was an apprentice-ship system. This came out of the medieval guild system and took on its capitalist form in industrial cities throughout the Western world around the middle of the nineteenth century, when those struggling for the public good convinced the capitalists – by social persuasion and public regulation – that they had long-term community responsibilities. The corpor-ations themselves began to realize that if they wanted quality products they needed to train their employees, starting as young as possible.

It wasn't until the globalist movement came along in the 1970s that corporations began to say they could no longer afford to train their workers, that in this new world they had no long-term obligations. Apprenticeship programs shrank or were dropped in most places, except in Germany. Interestingly enough, Germany is the only Western country to have come through the globalization era without a major employment crisis. Elsewhere, the training once done through apprenticeship was transferred over to schools and colleges, thus undermining the education and citizenship-preparation role of public education. Plus the corporations concentrated, successfully, on convincing governments to cut corporate taxes, thus undermining the possibility of funding the training programs they now expect from the public sector. This is only a partial explanation for the crisis in education, growing functional illiteracy and a sense of confused direction in public school systems. But it is one of the explanations.

In Canada we have the added element of a commodities-dependent economy in which corporations function in northern or isolated areas near small, isolated populations, in good part Aboriginal. Clearly, an apprenticeship program could play an important role. But to make that work serious consultation with local communities would be needed. And that in turn would require a critical mass of Aboriginals in middle and senior managerial positions.

Even if there were both managerial and on-site jobs available in acceptable numbers, and solid apprenticeship programs to make this work, we would still be talking about jobs related to the "exploit and move on" mentality of the industry. Equally, if not more important, Aboriginals want their share of the business itself.

That is the third part, the third desire. Equity. This is where power and long-term money lies. And this exploitation is taking place on their territory.

Fourth, it is through equity that they will gain the influence to introduce different business models. What could that mean? Well, take the example of the archipelago of Haida Gwaii off the Pacific coast. The Weyerhaeuser corporation was cutting down first-growth trees at a furious pace. They aimed at clearing out these valuable trees within ten years. The Haida had instead a long-term, sustainable approach. They saw and see themselves as an integral part of Haida Gwaii; they plan on staying and expect their descendants will stay. Their plan was not to maximize short-term profits and then leave. As for the local loggers, they had always sided with their employers – whoever owned the company – against the Haida. What changed everything was the publication of a credible report demonstrating that Weyerhaeuser did indeed plan to clean out the first-growth trees within ten years, then move on. The loggers were deeply disturbed. They talked among themselves and suddenly realized that they had more in common with the First Nations than with their employers. They also wanted to stay on Haida Gwaii, wanted their children to live there. And so they switched sides, supporting the Haida against their own employers. Like the Haida, they wanted a smarter approach, which meant a different approach.

Governments are only beginning to understand this, if at all. For so long they have been the loyal servants of the commodities corporations, handing off the Crown's rights in the most agreeable, collaborationist of ways. The last few years have seen an intensifying of this cozy relationship. The principal aim of our elected government seems to have become to serve the leadership of the commodities sector by dismantling decades of environmental legislation, removing any troublesome research from within government and funding industry-friendly research and infrastructure. No doubt the prime minister and ministers will eventually retire to comfortable jobs, board seats and consultancy contracts in the same sector. Don't think of this as raw corruption. Think of it rather as over-the-top ideology. The industry is being offered more than it could have imagined possible. Sometimes more than it believes wise.

Gordon Campbell came to power in British Columbia in 2001 determined to fight First Nations' progress. He was going to hold a referendum to justify undoing the Nisga'a agreement. Then he was visited by business leaders who explained that they didn't want that kind of fight. And so he watered down his referendum and actually became somewhat cooperative when it came to treaty negotiations, which was quite revolutionary for a B.C. premier. Years later you can see small signs of what is possible. For example, in March 2013 the B.C. government announced that the law-enforcement arms of two ministries – Forestry and Environment – would share authority with the Haida Nation on Haida Gwaii. The provincial government's group of compliance and enforcement civil servants on the archipelago will now include someone named by the Haida. And that group will be largely autonomous. Peter Lantin, president of the Council of the Haida Nation, argued this way: "Haida values are embedded into the day-to-day operations of managing the forests and streams." But this is only one small initiative. It needs to be duplicated all over the country.

From the point of view of the business world and the government, it should also be said that the general atmosphere has changed. The situation of indigenous people on several continents is now a common topic of conversation.

The relationship between the environment, indigenous people and commodities extraction is on the agenda everywhere. Companies are increasingly nervous about being caught in embarrassing situations. In my travels, I hear what people are saying about Canada around the world. I hear it repeatedly, from every direction. We had a respectable reputation, a positive reputation. The negative side of the balance has been growing rapidly. Our reputation has probably never been lower. A great deal of that has to do with our handling of the oil sands, mining, forestry, the environment and the situation of indigenous people.

Go on, huff and puff with indignation. If it makes you feel better, go right ahead and point out that the Europeans have conveniently forgotten their own recent past and are now uncomfortable with the old exploitation methods that once inspired them. See how far that gets you. True, their public actions are laced with hypocrisy. True, our Aboriginal stories of mistreatment cannot be compared to the war, violence, massacres and slavery seen in the United States, Mexico, Central and South America, and the Caribbean, or even Australia. But there is no honour to be had from those comparisons. It is true that much of what was done in those places was actively backed by the parents and grandparents of today's earnest, well-intentioned Europeans. It is also true that today's horror stories of mining in Latin America can be traced to the venality of their local governments. But that changes nothing. Attributing virtue to yourself is a form of self-delusion. The fact is that people around the world don't like what they are hearing about Canada.

Perhaps these outsiders don't know much about us and our realities. Perhaps they are indeed self-serving and hypocritical.

That simply doesn't matter. The indigenous peoples' situation is real. Our incapacity to face that situation with humility and active goodwill damages our reputation around the world.

Countries need their reputations for everything from diplomacy to business to investment. We can't afford to damage ours in this way.

# XIII

# THE RIGHT TO BE DIVIDED

There were those who seemed to take comfort, during the dramatic events of 2012–2013, in what they saw as fundamental divisions among First Nations peoples. They saw arguments within the Assembly of First Nations, some chiefs going to meetings with the government, others boycotting. A few even seemed to be using the situation to begin campaigning for the next AFN election. Outside observers seemed to feel that the national chief was being weakened by this internal situation, as well as by the young people in the streets, the remarkable expansion of the Idle No More movement, and the attention paid to Chief Spence and elder Raymond Robinson on a liquid diet on Victoria Island on the Ottawa River, in sight of the Parliament Buildings.

If you think of the First Nations movement that way – as a single voice for a monolithic group – then it is indeed divided. But it is not monolithic and has never wanted to be. Its strengths through history have come precisely from its multiple cultures and varied points of view. Does that make a national chief's life easy? Absolutely not. Ask Phil Fontaine, to name only one of the recent remarkable national chiefs. This is

Chief Spence with supporters. © Fred Chartrand/The Canadian Press.

one of the toughest political jobs in Canada: it's tough leading the First Nations movement, and it's tough dealing with the various Canadian governments.

What the standard political strategist sees as divisive weakness can equally be seen as a sign of strength. After all, Canadians in general are politically, even philosophically, divided. People living on the same street feel strongly and differently about at least three political parties and various specific issues. Isn't that the norm in a healthy society? Only dictatorships insist on agreement. Only weak groups are dependent on an artificially maintained solidarity in order to survive.

To take that a step further: the multiplicity of strategies and ideas among First Nations peoples is one of the signs of their growing strength. Look at the new leadership. The now former national chief, Shawn A-in-chut Atleo, is an impressive part of the new wave. Yes, he represents a point of view, one that saw him easily elected to a second term. Yes, other young leaders have other ideas. Yes, there are rival points of view. Yes, he has now resigned. What's wrong with all that? The Aboriginal world is burgeoning with ideas. Yes, there are differences between various First Nations and between regions. Gosh. That sounds like politics in Canada. Isn't the richness of ideas a strength?

Yes, there are serious differences of opinion, for example over the 2014 proposed Aboriginal education act. I'll come back to this. But these differences began from a point of agreement. Virtually everyone was in agreement that the government was attempting to dictate conditions and hold on to power. The differences were over whether it was better to begin with a preliminary acceptance or a preliminary refusal, in both cases to be followed by a tough negotiation.

Another example: during the winter of 2012–2013 you could read about Idle No More outflanking the AFN on the radical left and therefore weakening the national chief in his negotiations with the prime minister. But it could also be argued that if the government were to use the old strategies of divide and conquer and to succeed in discrediting the AFN leadership, well then Ottawa would have opened the way to a more radical leadership. The whole range of indigenous leaders would become increasingly bitter and angry about such manipulations.

This may well be what is now happening. Would the business community not feel that the government had mismanaged the situation? Would Canadians as a whole not become increasingly disturbed and embarrassed? And would they eventually punish politicians who had failed to bring this situation to a fair conclusion?

# XIV

# MOVING TO THE STREETS

What of Idle No More? Is it a sign of our historic moment?
Many people have noticed that among Canadians
only the indigenous youth went onto the streets in large
numbers to protest the 2012 omnibus bills. Everyone else
seemed afraid to: The NGOs. The unions. The various political movements. Do they fear for their jobs? The legal status
of their organization? Their funding? Their respectability as
middle-class players? Only the Aboriginals, some people say,
have nothing to lose.

Is this true? It could be seen in quite a different way.
Perhaps this commitment is another sign of growing power
and self-confidence. After all, by going onto the streets,
indigenous peoples have taken a leadership position. It isn't
fashionable to say this these days, but a willingness to go into
the streets shows a commitment to democracy. And Canadian
democracy, like so many others, was born in good part on the
streets in the middle of the nineteenth century.

It could be argued that the general alienation from our
formal system of democracy felt today by many people around
the world – one of the outcomes of the globalist period – has
pushed young people in particular back into the streets in a
way we have not seen since the 1930s. This is not like the

Indigenous youth and indigenous women are central to the comeback.
Here they are, leading the march on Ottawa on December 21, 2012.
© Nadya Kwandibens.

demonstrations of the 1960s, 1970s and 1990s, all of which
were driven by clear, specific, alternative views. What we are
seeing is a broadly conceived protest in countries where a
reigning logic of efficiency insists that money spent on the
public good is somehow a form of indulgence. There have
always been street protests, but if you look at Greece, Spain
and even the Occupy movement, something more fundamental is happening. These people are not organized in an
ideological way. They are not out there as union members
or as party members. Their approach seems to involve an
important rejection of democracy as we currently know it.
A rejection of the standard democratic electoral process by
a growing number of people. A rejection of today's mechanisms of political debate. A loss of respect for those elected. A

rejection of plebiscite-style false democracy. If this continues to grow it could lead anywhere, from the most negative to the intriguingly positive.

The Canadian position in all of this is surprisingly different. We have long had high levels of citizen engagement through volunteerism, and this includes high levels of youth engagement. That ought to represent a good non-partisan basis for democracy. Today the opposite seems to be the case.

Perhaps the presence of young people working on the ground increases their sense of alienation from formal politics, since they bear daily witness to what they feel is political failure – a failure to respond to the reality of people's lives, to how they can best live together and in the physical world, and worse still, a simple failure to understand what a society is, what it can be, how it can blossom in its physical reality. Instead there is an insistence on theories of economics and administrative efficiency in which citizens do not find themselves, in which there is little sense of society or place.

On the surface, Canada has a more successful economy with less unemployment than other Western countries. But again, this seems to have little effect on the growing rich–poor divide, except to the extent that our public education and public health-care systems remain reasonably strong and leave little room for the private sector. Many other countries have good public education and health-care systems, but a small number, including Canada, have an additional advantage because there is a fairly direct link between the importance of the private sector and the rise of a formal class system, which in turn accentuates the growth of a rich–poor divide.

One of the signs of a problem in our apparently successful

economy is that it has not produced a sense of optimism among young people, a sense of confidence in their working future. And there is almost no sense that our economy is the product of leadership or governmental management.

We know we are very fortunate. We are rich in commodities, particularly in oil and gas. This is luck. Fine, we might be skilful in exploiting our luck. But there is no natural link between this wealth and the sharing of it. The long anti-democratic, anti-environmental, anti-social-justice history of the commodities sector around the world is a constant reminder that even in a democracy it requires severe regulation – and that government is increasingly soft and compliant toward it. This is part of the general lack of confidence in public structures. You could say that there is a depressive link between governmental indulgence toward this industry and the decline of solid, full-time jobs, including benefits, for young people throughout the economy.

On the other hand, we have a continuing infusion of human energy from our long-established immigration/citizenship system. And in the 1990s, when the financial sector was deregulated in much of the world and our own banks, backed by the Conservatives, were pushing hard for deregulation in Canada, the middle-of-the-road Liberal government in power in Ottawa dragged its feet. Eventually it said no to the banks. So when the crisis came, we were saved.

Is our economic situation more complicated than all that? No doubt. But those are our basic strengths and the basic explanations for them: money in the ground, relatively egalitarian and inclusive immigration systems and public services, and long-standing conservative, as opposed to neo-conservative, financial regulations.

The first, most obvious point to be made here is that Aboriginal peoples are put at a disadvantage in all of these areas. That is, they are disadvantaged by laws, regulations, funding and institutionalized prejudice.

The second is that Canada has so far seen a far broader range of street movements than most countries.

It could be argued that Idle No More, the Occupy movement and the Quebec student movement all indicate a growing rejection of politics as we know it in Canada. They signal a rejection of political careerism and of the instrumentalized corruption that goes with it, but also a rejection of the increasing acceptance of social determinism – the return of the class system – that seems to be the natural accompaniment of this careerism. It is worth noting that, as part of the Canadian phenomenon, the Wall Street Occupy movement had its origins in Vancouver in *Adbusters* magazine.

But what exactly is being rejected? We have to keep thinking about that. For example, there is a growing loss of faith in what might be called managerialism. Here was an approach to social organization that was supposed to keep all of us, as well as our programs, on track. It clearly has not. If anything, it has combined a demeaning form of utilitarian determinism with a sapping of the citizen's sense of purpose. Why? Because it limits our actions to superficial but complex forms of organization, in which we become enmeshed and lose our ability to argue back.

All of this adds up to the rejection of a great deal more than a few policies or a political party. It suggests the rejection of a system that has dominated us for half a century with increasingly utilitarian assumptions about how societies should function – that is, not really as societies, but as a haphazard bundle of self-absorbed individuals driven by self-interest. The moment the governing elite thinks of society as a combination of self-interest and utilitarianism, you can be sure that attempts will be made to distract citizens from their demeaning situation by the cheap exploitation of populism and nationalism.

Populism becomes essential: bread and circuses; sports elevated from fun and exercise to patriotic purpose; military rhetoric. The most effective populist tool is fear. An inchoate fear of *the Other*. Authorities constantly suggesting that you will be murdered, raped, beaten up, blown up. Only constant vigilance (institutionalized fear of your fellow citizen) and punishment can save you. Security, not citizenship. Not a strengthening of the public good.

It means the loss of a sense of purpose and responsibility, the loss even of a sense of dignity, of citizen responsibility, of citizen power. After all, once you accept an ideology that places an abstract force like economic theory or race or divinity above the public good, you cannot help but reduce the feeling of human responsibility and human dignity. In that sense we have all been subjected over the last few years to a partial version of the alienating discourse that Aboriginals have lived with for over a century.

Again, let me give a precise example. Many people tried to interpret the Quebec student movement in the narrowest possible way. *It was merely about tuition in a province where taxes are high and tuition already low. It was an attack on the provincial government.* The then provincial Liberal government was so caught up in management arguments of relative costs and deliverables that it could never understand the message in the streets. The opposition – the Parti Québécois – attempted to co-opt the student movement. This was pure cynicism. They themselves, when last in power, had been the ones to introduce the higher tuition policies later taken up by the Liberals. Their co-opting strategy lasted only a few months after the 2012 election. How could it last? None of the parties were listening to what the students were attempting to articulate. None were trying to understand.

Now, let me bring this back to the specifics of Idle No More. Most people, people with positions in society, respectable people, people who have some degree of power and don't want to lose it, are in favour of discretion. They tend not to put their faces and their opinions on camera. And Canadians often think of themselves that way – earnest but discreet. This is odd because the history of Canadian democracy has not been particularly respectable. It has been shaped by ideas fought out in public debate. Somewhere in that process people usually find that they have to go into the streets. This was disastrously true of Papineau and Mackenzie, successfully true of LaFontaine and Baldwin. It has been true throughout our history when it comes to major issues. And it could be argued that by spending a lot of time in the streets, in public meetings, in political meetings, in citizen-led organizations, we have avoided the worst sorts of violence that have overtaken other Western countries. I can't think of another country so given to movements outside of the formal political structures. Much of the best progress in this country has come through this sort of engagement.

Think of the environmental movement: David Schindler on acid rain, David Suzuki, Maurice Strong. Think of the birth of the Canadian approach to foreign policy: Henri Bourassa, J.W. Dafoe. Women's rights: Nellie McClung and dozens of others. The end of capital punishment. The welcoming of large groups of refugees. And on and on. All of the issues were led from public platforms. From the streets.

The high levels of Canadian volunteerism are usually thought of as expressions of our earnest and discreet characters. In reality this engagement is part of the belief that changes can be made if citizens engage themselves and find non-official ways to lead.

There is one other interesting point. The Aboriginal leadership – whether in the AFN or Idle No More or coming from scattered, independent voices – is demonstrating a clear understanding of parliamentary democracy, far clearer perhaps than the NGOs and the professionals of political science. Aboriginal leaders understand that you must be willing to go into the streets and stay there if your cause is great.

The founders of Idle No More: Nina Wilson, Sylvia McAdam, Jessica Gordon and Sheela McLean, all from Saskatchewan. © www.idlenomore.ca.

What drove the creation of Idle No More were particular parts of two omnibus bills – C-38 and C-45. These contained dozens and dozens of changes to laws in all directions. The first key issue for Aboriginals in C-38 had to do with a massive weakening of regulations governing the use of Canadian waterways. They saw this as the lead-up to an assault on the environment. In other words, after a half century of consensus that we had to clean up rivers and lakes polluted by industrial and urban activity, here was an attempt by your elected government to reverse the trend and go back to polluting. But they also saw it as another one of those clever legal tricks to weaken or get around indigenous rights and responsibilities.

The second issue with C-38 had to do with the weakening of the Fisheries Act. That act was originally conceived to protect fish habitats and therefore fish. The omnibus bill removed protection of habitats; it talked only of fish, and in a largely commercial context. What this does is invert the purpose of the law. The original intent was positive and proactive: if you focus on fish habitats you set the context for a healthy fish population. You are setting a standard for healthier lakes and rivers, which provide drinking water and which host a diversity of plants and insects, of life in general. Animals are dependent on its health. We are all dependent on its health. By reducing the law to an object – fish – you make it negative and defensive. In legal terms, the crime must be committed before you can complain. You must arrive in court carrying, so to speak, a pile of rotting, infected fish. The damage is already done. In other words, the concept of a proactive policy in which we assume our long-term responsibilities, which in turn is central to any sensible environmental approach, is reduced to the old utilitarian model – minimalist and reactive. That approach has already produced a crisis in fish populations around the world. In this model, corporations used to have a VP Environmental and Social Affairs, inevitably a lawyer whose job it was to fight off the lawsuits after incidents like toxic spills. It is worth noting that, before it was gutted, our Fisheries Act was much admired in other countries.

In C-45 the issue is a weakening of the rules over the leasing out of land on reserves. The sense among First Nations is that this land-use change is aimed at undermining their control over their land as formalized in large part under the treaties. In the name of choice and the opportunity to make a buck in the short term, this proviso aims to create a patchwork of holdings on treaty land – held cooperatively or held more or less privately – and so lessen the influence of First Nations in commodity-rich areas. It does this by opening the door for individuals to effectively remove land from the common whole through leasing. Corporations would be able to take advantage of this patchwork. And, of course, this comes before the central question of treaty negotiations has been answered. To put it in historical terms, this could be seen as an old-fashioned attempt to create the legal structures for yet another land grab, this time disguised in market terminology: *Everyone should have a chance to make money by leasing out their land.*

In other words, this change in land-use rules is seen as a new version of the Manitoba Métis scrip crisis, in which land promised to the Métis in the 1870s, after Louis Riel's provisional government, was handed out so slowly that it undermined local society and had to be sold off to settlers from Ontario at rock-bottom prices. What is the resemblance to C-45 today? Imagine you are part of a community living on an isolated reserve. It is a poor place. There is the promise of a better situation if only the interminable treaty negotiations could be completed. But there is no sign of that. They have been dragging on for years, perhaps decades. Suddenly one of the negotiating parties – the government – uses its power to change the ground rules. They undermine the treaty process by making it possible for the land-holding rules to be eased. You see that under those rules you could lease out your piece of the land. You are poor. Almost any one of us would do that.

You realize, of course, that the government's manoeuvre is dishonest. They are betraying the Honour of the Crown, first by prolonging the negotiations and so worsening the effects of the poverty; second by confusing the land-holding system in order to undermine the negotiating position of the community. Is this a deeply unethical conflict of interest on the part of those in power? Absolutely. A lack of respect for citizens? Yes. An attempt to undermine the treaty negotiations? Of course. A betrayal of the Honour of the Crown? Yes.

And why? Well, there is always the desire of Canadian authorities to reduce the amount of land held by indigenous people and, failing that, to weaken their authority over their land. This desire is driven in part by the generic idea of power. But Aboriginal land has always also represented potential wealth for others – agricultural land, forestry land, rights of way. This has not changed. Where impoverished bands hold sway, there may well be mining opportunities. These new land-holding rules aimed at a patchwork holding system are a way to exclude one group from this wealth – indigenous peoples – and shift the advantage to the old combine of urban-commodities corporations and political parties.

As always, the government's actions are disguised in legal obscurity. And of course, there have been other omnibus bills over the last half century. But nothing like this – at least not in Canada. So perhaps it isn't surprising that people put at a great disadvantage for more than a century and now gathering back strength should react strongly to this return of the old exploitative ways of Canadian governments.

Aboriginals have a clear memory of this kind of betrayal by the authorities. The rest of us are less conscious, less prepared to believe or understand that the public good is under direct attack. We are more naive. Is it surprising that public leadership on these issues is taken up by the indigenous community?

# XV

# AN OMNIBUS IS A BUS

We are meant to be living in a parliamentary democracy. Central to this system is the power of Parliament through the confidence it gives and takes away from governments. But the other equally important power is Parliament's obligation to examine, one by one, each proposed change or initiative.

In most cases, that process of examination is far more important than the technicality of a parliamentary vote. Of course there must be votes in order to convert proposed legislation into law. The vote is the punctuation of the democratic parliamentary sentence. The sentence itself is the debate. The vote finishes the sentence. But the content that produces the punctuation is the debate.

Why one by one? So that the representatives of the people can focus on the topic of each law. This matter of focus is particularly important. It is how the intelligence of democracy works. We do not merely receive leadership, as in authoritarian regimes. We constantly consider leadership. And so the topic of each proposed law is focused on and examined, clause by clause. Time is taken. This is a slow process. It is meant to be slow. Speed, except in an extreme crisis, is not a characteristic of democracy, and certainly not of parliamentary democracy.

It takes a great deal of time to flesh out ideas, intents, positives and negatives, and to flush them out into the broad public domain so that citizens hear about them and have time to think and consider and gradually express themselves.

We all know that these parliamentary powers – of bestowing and taking away confidence in a government, of examining and deciding on laws – have been weakened over recent decades by the rise of highly formalized political parties. The real power has slipped more or less to the prime minister's office and the bureaucracy. And this is more or less the case in parliamentary democracies all over the world.

Commentators on power and those who exercise it have gradually and correspondingly downplayed the importance of debate and discussion. More precisely, they have denigrated language as the means by which we work out what to do, reducing it to the declarative, the assertive, the formulaic. And so they have increasingly criticized both Parliament and parliamentarians for wasting the time of the experts, who just want to get on with running things. In other words, those who believe their job is to be efficient and to reward efficiency criticize Parliament for its inefficiency. This innocuous argument may sound vaguely familiar. It is, of course, the latest version of Mussolinian corporatism. Making the trains run on time, as they used to say. It is a rejection of functioning democracy in favour of narrow delivery systems. This in turn can be made less boring by the distraction of heroic leaders, which increasingly means celebrity leaders, or leaders who affect the characteristics of celebrities. If they can't make themselves appear heroic, they can rely on the mechanisms of plebiscite government and, as I mentioned a few pages ago, on the cheap exploitation of populism and nationalism.

The democratic position can be summarized in two points. First, parliamentary power carries with it the power of the people through the government's having the confidence of the House. Second, the idea of giving and taking away that parliamentary confidence may work differently today because of the formalization of political parties, but the principle of confidence remains a fundamental characteristic of parliamentary democracy. To see it fully in action you need only elect a minority government. Prime ministers and their offices hate minorities, as do the technocrats – whether public or private sector. Curiously enough, so do most commentators. They are all addicted to the corporatist or Mussolinian idea of efficiency. What this tells us is that the ability to examine pieces of legislation slowly, one by one, is probably even more important today in an era of technocracy; that is, an era when experts are resistant to being examined by generalists. There is now a desperate need to parse the mechanisms of power.

So this is a time when ideologues can hide behind the dominant mythology of efficiency in order to run roughshod over Parliament, as if they were acting in the public interest. How? By saving time and therefore money. How? By not wasting time on debate. On words. On ideas. On consideration. The impatient taxpayer overrides the concerned citizen, as if self-interest overrides the obligation of the citizenry and of their elected representatives to protect and advance the public good.

It is true that a transparent parliamentary discussion of legislation may not lead to governmental defeats in Parliament when the moment comes to vote. But these debates do lead to public awareness. And that can make a government's situation untenable. Some might say that that also is no longer so, that no one follows parliamentary debates. In fact it all depends on which debate, on how these debates are treated by the debaters and by the press. Taken seriously, they can have a serious effect. And even when they seem to be being ignored, ideas are nevertheless being brought into the light. You could say that debate liberates ideas from the confines of the inward-looking specialist processes and from the ideologues' insistence on superficial phrases of purpose and inevitability. Like a flock of game birds hiding in the long grass of expertise, ideas are indeed flushed out by debate and forced to fly up into the public air.

We never really know what will happen after that, how we the public will embrace certain ideas and reject others, fixing on them and shooting them down. Or how we then decide to punish those in power who have ignored our indications of displeasure. That openness is part of the citizen's mindset, of the indirect effect of parliamentary democracy.

The plebiscite or referendum system of government is quite different. It is the Napoleonic or heroic model, in which the government assumes a black-and-white version of power. This always involves marginalizing all other competing institutions, such as Parliament. It also means that power must override authority, which is the domain of the head of state, or, in the Canadian case, the authority of the Crown – that is, the people – which resides with the effective head of state, the governor general. In other words, in a plebiscite system of government, the citizen is left to vote once in a general election – for or against – then to sit back for four or five years, leaving those in power with a generalized mandate to do what they want. It is a form of direct democracy, if you like. The exact opposite of parliamentary or indirect democracy.

---

Let me put this another way. Direct democracy without strong countervailing forces is not democracy. That's why the U.S. system of government limits the direct power of the president with three – originally four – strong counterweights: the Senate, the House of Representatives and the Supreme Court. The state governments used to be more of a counterweight. Now you might say they simply have different responsibilities.

This comparison of Canada with the United States is important because the accelerating use by Canadian governments of gigantic omnibus bills as catch-all mechanisms is taken directly from the U.S. Congress. The Canadian omnibus bills are now presented as Budget Implementation Acts, as if they were coherent outcomes of the budget. In fact, much of the content is not budgetary, or only marginally so. They are policy items. And there is no common or integrated theme.

Worse still, the detailed examination of the contents is controlled by the Finance Committee, while the subjects being examined are about the environment or transportation or whatever. These are very different policy items requiring separate acts of Parliament in order to permit proper debate and proper examination in the appropriate committee – in other words, proper fleshing out of the different ideas in each act.

The concept of a vast potpourri of ideas bundled up in a budget bill comes directly from the Congress's approach to budgeting. Their budget bills are a grab bag of items. But in their case there is a good reason. The American budget bills are the outcome of long, hard-fought battles in Congress and Congress committees over government spending. The outcome may be a cynical compromise – a bridge offered here in return for an airport there. It may be filled with contradictions and basely political. But it is the result of a fully fleshed-out debate and committee examination. It is the result of a balanced democratic process.

The Canadian imitation is completely different. It is all about removing any possible counterweights, about eliminating most debate. It constricts committee examination. Canadian omnibus bills have been turned into an expression of raw power – the will of the government organized to minimize the role of Parliament and to short-circuit public debate. The democratic function is eliminated as a reality. What remains is pro-forma voting. A pastiche of parliamentary democracy.

And so the form now taken by Canadian omnibus bills does not belong to parliamentary democracy. It belongs to the referendum or plebiscite system.

Does that mean there can be no omnibus bills in a parliamentary system? Not at all. A small omnibus bill with a coherent policy theme can fit into parliamentary traditions. A massive catch-all omnibus bill disguised as a Budget Implementation Act belongs to the plebiscite system. In between there is less clarity. With Bills C-38 and C-45, we are clearly in Napoleonic plebiscite territory.

———

Let me explain this situation a third way.

Some people argue that we should all relax. Not only does parliamentary debate not matter, but omnibus bills have been around for almost half a century; were invented by Pierre

Trudeau with his 1968 Criminal Law Amendment Act. Every government since has used the omnibus mechanism as a sensible way to speed up and make sense of the arcane parliamentary process.

This is an intentional misrepresentation, which is to say, it is a lie.

What is true is that governments have long created packages of laws, probably since 1888, when two railway agreements were linked. The point is obvious: parliamentary omnibus bills were about putting together legislation linked by a single theme. Trudeau's 1968 law was concentrated on reforming criminal law, with a special focus on expanding personal rights and privacy. In 1971 there was a major departmental restructuring. In 1982 there was an energy sector act.

In 1988 a Liberal speaker of the House approved the Free Trade Act, ruling that an omnibus bill must have one basic principle or purpose that ties together the proposed enactments and thereby renders the bill intelligible for parliamentary purposes. Why mention that the speaker was a Liberal? Because the government was Conservative, which highlights just how non-partisan the ruling was.

Even within this principle, Parliament has often been uncomfortable with such limitations on the people's right to have their representatives debate legislation. So in 1982 the House forced the division of the omnibus bill into eight separate pieces of legislation.

These are not technical fights. They are fundamental issues of democracy. They tell us why the omnibus bills of the last few years are radically different from what came before.

The plebiscite or referendum form of government to which I have been referring first developed into a modern alternative to democracy under Napoleon. The idea was that the legitimacy of government would be transferred from the people to the government via periodic mass votes. In between there was no need for debate. There was no need to parse policy.

This approach was refined by authoritarian governments throughout the nineteenth century and on into the 1930s. By then it had been formalized as a characteristic of populist governments, an approach now associated with Argentina's Peronism.

Is this really relevant to what is happening in Canada? Is the change in the type of omnibus bill really so great?

The answer lies in straightforward comparisons. For example, the single-theme omnibus bills of the late-nineteenth century through the twentieth averaged seventy pages in length. The recent omnibus bills average three hundred pages. In 2012, Bill C-38 – in which the stripping of protection from fish habitats is mixed up with unemployment insurance eligibility – was 425 pages long with 753 clauses changing 69 unrelated laws. In the same year, Bill C-45 was 457 pages long and used 516 clauses to amend 64 laws. These ranged from stripping the environmental protection from rivers and lakes to altering public sector pensions.

The outcome is clear. In twelve months, Parliament was bullied into radically altering 133 largely unrelated laws through two acts. There was very little debate.

This was a direct negation of our democratic system. Napoleon would have approved. Mussolini would have been jealous. Peron would have been filled with admiration.

———

Please forgive this bit of boring political science 101. But the odd thing is that the political scientists remained pretty silent during the events of 2012. Is it that they have fallen into a cynical mindset? Or have they become so obsessed by themselves as scientists that they have channelled their intellect into a microscopic measurement of power – the way the television camera has reduced the apparent complexity of hockey by fixating on the puck? And so, in an academic version of the Wayne Gretzky dictum about skating not to where the puck is but to where the puck will go, most of them seem to follow what happens rather than seeing what should or could or ought to happen in the context of the system. Or perhaps most of them have simply lost the habit of intervening in public, as if it were beneath their dignity. If so, this is part of the crisis of academics withdrawing from public commitment and so betraying the central purpose of their tenure, which exists for the precise purpose of giving them the independence to intervene publicly without the risk of being fired.

Some NGOs did raise their voice. A bit. Rather primly. Very quietly. Certainly not insistently. Rarely in the street. Civil society too has become a world of professionals. Technocrats for the good, but nevertheless technocratic. Or are they afraid that the new rules surrounding charitable status – without which it is difficult to raise money – actually represent a politicization of the sector by the current government? That if they speak up clearly on public issues they risk having their charitable status removed or finding themselves being audited every year, at great expense, to say nothing of the waste of time? Is this really happening to respectable civil society organizations? Yes it is. Has the arm's-length relationship between political power and public administration – the firewall that has been central to the functioning of modern Canadian society – actually been removed? There is evidence to this effect.

I should add that this concept of the arm's-length relationship has been what separates a small group of democratic countries from the many authoritarian regimes and from those weaker democracies that believe political power carries the right to politicize public programming by helping your friends and punishing your enemies. Countries that believe in the arm's-length principle have more active and outspoken citizens, a more vibrant democracy, a fairer society. If, as it appears, Canada is being shifted from the arm's-length model to one in which power gives all rights, then we are at a dangerous turning point.

———

It was Aboriginals – through the Idle No More movement, through the frustration of youth, through a wave of new voices across the country, through their AFN leadership – who raised their voices, went into the street, took personal action, seized every opportunity to speak up.

Their message? Our system is being changed in a profound way. Democratic permission has not been given for such changes. Parliament has been denied its fundamental responsibility of free speech; that is, of normal, full debate. And this to an unprecedented degree.

As I have already said, this latest move of public interventions by indigenous peoples needs to be seen as a sign of self-confidence, a sign of their comeback, of their willingness to take the lead.

In situations like these, all of us who do not go into the

streets, who do not directly engage in some verbal or physical way, begin by seeing ourselves as outsiders or simple observers. Perhaps as concerned observers. Some among us then lose interest. We go back to our daily routine. Others become annoyed. They see themselves as free-floating individuals. Whatever they do, whatever their routine is, trumps the actions and needs of everyone else. In a sense they have inverted the ethical idea that a society is a place in which the actions of an individual should not harm other individuals. The broad, humanist idea that individualism is about involvement in the shared public good is thus reduced by the self-absorbed and easily annoyed among us to mean that we must not be inconvenienced in our habits. And these sacred habits may vary from our daily needs to go driving and shopping to our unimpeded right to serve our own interests, even if fellow citizens are left to suffer. In this twisted scenario, those who are protesting against wrong being done to them or who are willing to make sacrifices for the broader public good are converted by the annoyed, self-obsessed observer into selfish people getting in the way of average citizens who wish to go about their normal lives undisturbed.

What we saw developing around Idle No More was that many Canadians, not normally involved in Aboriginal issues, began to feel themselves involved and concerned. They began to see themselves as somehow part of what was being said in the streets. True, they did not at first get up and go into the streets. But in conversations everywhere you could hear people worrying, somehow trying to understand the arguments being put forward. This could indicate a real step forward in the national psyche. And remember, it all happened during the winter. For Canadians, there is something particularly convincing about people going into the streets in the winter and staying there.

When I talked at the time with young First Nations leaders across the country – professors, businesspeople, professionals, writers, politicians – they were excited about Idle No More. Not necessarily by the organization itself, which might morph into something else or into many new things. And not necessarily because they believed it had the answers or could succeed in some dramatic way. But because it showed the breadth and depth of commitment in their communities. A grassroots commitment to the public good. And it showed a widespread determination by a new generation to be heard, to be part of a serious discussion of the future.

This generation feels that it is on the move. Its members are not prepared to live with disappointment. What if Canada, through its various leaders, fails to seize this opportunity? Fails to listen? To discuss? Fails to work, through a broad, transparent negotiation, toward a sense of resolution, a sense of concrete respect and creative progress? What if Canada wraps itself in an omnibus approach to power? Plebiscitary? In effect Napoleonic? Well then, Canada will have forced this burgeoning Aboriginal leadership into a renewed sense of exclusion. It will have produced – quite unnecessarily – a whole new phenomenon of bitterness. And this anger and disappointment, this loss of hope, will be solidly built upon a foundation of one hundred and fifty years of betrayal, anger and disappointment. Is this really what Canadians want? To confirm to young Aboriginals that their only possible relationship with Canadian society is one of negativity and bitterness? The obligation of those with power is to avoid such a situation. If they do not, we will all suffer greatly. The obligations of citizens is to make it clear that Aboriginal issues are central to our public concerns, that we want them dealt with in a fully democratic context of openness and justice, that we will vote accordingly.

The flow of history is reinforcing the position of Aboriginal peoples. This is a historic and a human opportunity. To attempt to deny or to turn back such a moment of creativity would be self-destructive for Canada.

# XVI

# BOYS WHO CAN'T COMMIT

The omnibus bill crisis has raised a far broader question, one that has dogged Canada for a century and a half.

Our governments will not engage in Aboriginal matters. Not really. Not fully. Not with enthusiasm for the possibility of reconciliation, let alone restitution. In fact, we haven't ever had a government that has put its mind to trying to understand what the concept of reconciliation means, let alone how to transform the concept into a concrete fact. Paul Martin is a bit of an exception to the rule, but he wasn't in office long enough to become a functioning prime minister of a real government. He certainly never got to the stage of turning his Kelowna Accord into a mainstream reality that could inhabit the mainstream Canadian imagination.

And so it follows that our governments, one after the other, have not been able to bring themselves to break away from the European urban–rural myth of what constitutes a nation state or a country in order to treat the "commodities belt" – the northern two-thirds of Canada – as a real part of the country. To not treat it as just a source of commodities, colonial territories that will make those of us in the south rich. There has not been a real effort to include those areas as an integral part of Canada, as a place where citizens live. Over the last few years our government has been talking more than ever of northerners becoming rich only if southern miners are allowed to do what they want in the north.

Over the decades our governments have, of course, had moments of enthusiasm for northern projects. Canada was the driving force behind the creation of the Arctic Council. Then we lost interest. The Scandinavians had to take over as the effective leaders. We refused to invest money in its becoming a real force – a body with structures and policies. The chairmanship rotates. When our turn comes, we make it clear that we won't do anything with this responsibility, except encourage mining.

Canada was also the leading force in the creation of the virtual circumpolar University of the Arctic. But then, early in this century, the circumpolar world came on board and we were faced with the threat of having to take responsibility for our idea. Worse, we might have had to demonstrate our commitment by hosting the university in Canada. My god! Money might have had to be spent on strengthening our northern society. So of course we backed off as fast as we could, and Finland, so much bigger, so much richer than Canada, took over the leadership. The Canadians who had led in putting it all together moved to northern Finland, where people understand what a northern policy looks like.

Worse still, Canada remains the only circumpolar country without an Arctic university. I wrote about this in *A Fair Country*. And I'll keep repeating it. Why is there no Arctic university? Apparently we can't afford one. Greenland can, population 56,840. Iceland can, population 324,000. Norway can, population 5 million. Finland can, population 5.5 million. Sweden can, population 9.5 million. Canada, population 34 million,

G7 member, cannot. Besides, we don't have a large enough northern population to justify a university. Except that our northern population is one of the largest among the circumpolar countries.

The real difference seems to be that the southern-based leadership of the other circumpolar countries actually believes that their north is an integral part of their country. It's a small detail, but one worth considering.

On the positive side it should be added that an Arctic research station is being installed in the central Arctic at Cambridge Bay. It is projected to open in 2017. This is a big investment in an important building and a good initiative.

However, this plan was preceded in 2012 by the shutting down of the smaller, but well established, Eureka research station in the high Arctic on Ellesmere Island. Why no research station in the Arctic for five years? And Cambridge Bay is thirteen hundred kilometres to the south of Eureka. Why abandon high Arctic research on, for example, climate change? Why couldn't Eureka have been the northern outpost of the new station in Cambridge Bay? Why was Eureka shut in a rush? The financial savings argument is not convincing. Is it because it was independent-minded and focused on climate change, which the government doesn't want to deal with? Was it because the government wants to switch from independent research to applied research requested by industry? Designed by industry? Of course applied research is a good thing. But should it replace more fundamental work? Why is it either/or? And should taxpayers be paying for work that could be paid for by corporations? Besides, there are two kinds of applied research. There is the big industrial focus. But more importantly there is the precise applied research needed for our Artic communities. And there we are falling way behind.

There is another, even more important question. Is the Cambridge Bay station to be peopled mainly by scientists who live there full time? Is it to become a hub of northern-centred research and thought? This is what we need. Or is it to be a more sophisticated version of what we have already – a well-equipped place for researchers from southern universities to use as a base for their annual three months up north? These southern scientists now control northern research. Their southern universities get the benefit in reputation and funding from this colonial relationship to the north. And they stand in the way of the development of a northern-based approach and the development of a northern research community, which would include northerners, northern students and northern approaches, including Inuit concepts, known as the principles of Inuit Qaujimajatuqangit.

When the research program was finally announced in August 2014, it was focused on technology. As for the investment in actual research, it came down to a miserable $2 million a year. The whole program is based on the hope of investment by industry, for industry. This suggests that the research station is more of a rental opportunity for southerners and corporations than the beginning of a northern-based research community.

The government's four research priorities are resource development, transportation (relating to resource development and defence), marine safety (again relating to resource development and defence) and finally community infrastructure. There probably won't be much private money for this fourth priority, almost as if it were an afterthought.

It is a question of policy. And, as with all indigenous policies, it is a matter of mindset. Of narrative. This could of course be altered.

Central to a healthy change in narrative would be the context created by an Arctic university. Why is such a large investment being made in a research centre – a good idea and the proof that the money exists for intellectual development in the Arctic – without any move toward a university?

Is the answer that this is what the southern universities want? What corporations want? Is there no commitment in Ottawa to the development of a northern-based community of learning and thinking?

If these are fair questions, then they take us back to the central issue of our unfulfilled engagement in the north: Why do we lose interest so easily? Because the old colonial dreams – so much part of our provincial and federal structures – reassert themselves. In the colonial mind, the north is a place from which wealth is to be extracted, including the wealth of knowledge. Corporations and universities based in the south continually remind us of this, and they lobby the government hard to ensure that Ottawa doesn't go all soft and romantic and start treating the northern two-thirds of Canada as anything other than outlying territories where the commodities are. Only four or five years ago there was great enthusiasm in Ottawa for social and basic state investment and development in the Arctic. Lots of specifics were announced. Slowly they evaporated until now little is left except mining projects and this research centre. Even the military dreams are largely gone. The first elements to evaporate had to do with strengthening the reality of northern peoples as citizens of Canada. Why would they want to be treated as citizens when they can be given a job in a mine?

Is this fair? Am I suggesting something romantic or nationalistic that doesn't include jobs? Don't I believe that northerners have the right to mines and the jobs they offer and the training that will produce the jobs? The sensible answer is always the same: the choice should not be between being ignored and accepting jobs on someone else's conditions. There is a bigger picture filled with social conditions, rights, a broader sense of the economy that includes people and the environment. And, of course, there is that central question of high-quality education, properly funded. If you build a strategy that includes these elements, to say nothing of working closely with northern citizens, the way to shape economic development will emerge.

Let me take this argument down to the most basic level. We southerners tell ourselves that we want to travel east, west, south. Not north. We want to go to Paris, London, the Caribbean, Florida, Hawaii, Bali. Fine. But at one level, these are the dreams of the insecure. Not fair, you say. Of course there is nothing wrong with visiting cathedrals and palaces. And why not lie on a beach in the sun? Fine. But that is not the point. Ask most Canadians: Have you been to the Arctic? A look of panic. It's so difficult to get there! Actually, just go online and buy a ticket on First Air. It's so expensive! Actually, no more expensive than Europe. My god, where would I stay? In a Co-op hotel, motel, B&B. Summer or winter, the Arctic is one of the most exciting places in the world, one of the most surprising, one of the most beautiful. Inuit are among the most welcoming.

What then underpins these myths that drive most Canadians away from the Aboriginal reality? I believe it is the incredibly powerful reality of a colonial mindset. That sounds a bit facile. Is it unnecessarily insulting?

Not really. Think about our references when we talk about ourselves. We don't seem to be able to get ourselves beyond the European model – that model in which there is no Aboriginal component. And where there is no vast northern element in which nature dominates. We don't seem to be able to think of ourselves and Canada outside of the European model in which the urban is superior and the countryside feeds the urban. Of course we know that there is some rough nature lying somewhere out there, but it exists only for one-way exploitation or for the pleasurable distraction of the urbanite. And so we cannot bring ourselves to make the effort to make the northern two-thirds of our country strong. We do not make the long-term strategic and real investments in community in the north. This is the single most depressing thing about Canada because it is – I repeat – a constant reminder of a colonial state of mind.

# XVII

# LEADERSHIP

The indigenous situation in Canada may be complex. But the road to improving our shared situation is not particularly complicated.

Go back to the first pages of this book. It is disingenuous to dwell on the differences of opinion between indigenous leaders, claiming that what is holding things up is how divided and fractious they are. This is an excuse for doing nothing. Now pause. Step back. Remove yourself from the standard mainstream language and arguments surrounding indigenous peoples. Take a cool, disinterested look at our history. Think of yourself as a representative sent in by the United Nations or an international court of justice. Place yourself differently in the whole debate.

For example, imagine that drinking water mysteriously begins poisoning people in Walkerton, Ontario. Such a catastrophe could not happen in Canada, in a well-run, middle-class democracy. But just for discussion's sake, let's go along with this fable.

People die. People are crippled for life. Officials deny responsibility. They do not act. They are so incompetent that not only do they cause the crisis, but through denial of the possible causes, they also prolong it and cause more deaths. Impossible. Or rather: Impossible!

All the same, let's imagine what would happen next. Would the federal government, the Ontario government, the people of Canada say that this crisis was caused by dishonesty and drink? And therefore that the problem can't be resolved as long as these governance problems remain, and, what's more, as long as there is no unity of thought and policy in the town? Would we say, "First the people of Walkerton need to get their act together. We help those who help themselves. In fact, we'll just leave them all to stew until they come up with a clear position stating what they want. Oh, and clean water seems very expensive. Whatever we do must not stretch existing government budgets. Of course we understand that children are dying. But budgets must be respected. And one more thing: all government actions – should we choose to help – will be subjected to the long-standing methodologies of two departments. It's true that these methods have a long history of failure. But that's the fault of the citizens who seem incapable of living up to departmental standards by following departmental methods.

"Since these experienced departments know so well what they're doing, even though they usually fail, there's no need for transparency in their actions. For the good of all citizens, the whole problem will be dealt with top down, with little or no consultation, as if Walkerton's citizens were wards of the state. If they have poisonous water, they deserve to be treated as wards.

"Finally, any disagreement from the local community, in particular their leaders, will be taken as proof of recalcitrance and will immediately result in a battle to the death in the law courts. Federal and provincial lawyers will struggle mightily against Walkerton's citizens in renal failure. And why? The authority of the state must be defended. And taxpayers' money must be saved. Of course it must."

Now relax. This is only a fable. It would never happen. And if the citizens of Walkerton were poisoned by their drinking water, even if it was the fault of their own officials and the result of cutbacks by a ruling provincial party that would later take these methods to Ottawa, our government would immediately act to fix the problem. They would ensure that everyone got clean water, whatever it cost; that health care at its best was available for those affected. As for any criminal activity or failure, it would be referred to the legal system. We wouldn't let that get in the way of the well-being of citizens. The main issue would be health and clean water. That is a basic matter of the public good. As is housing; prevention of poverty, hunger, and suicide epidemics; education; social services; and a few other things. To fail to ensure clean drinking water would be a clear failure of Canadian civilization and therefore of Canadian leaders. We would lose all confidence in them.

———

Why, then, does federal inaction, and the lack of integrated strategies and federal funding, so often rely on the excuse that there are differences of opinion among Aboriginal leaders and they must get their act together before the government plays its part?

For a start, there has been remarkable continuity in the discourse of Aboriginal leaders for a hundred and fifty years. The central lines of argument have not varied. They have been explaining the same things about our relationship, about how we can live together, about what treaties mean. Read the 1910

Mistahimaskwa "Big Bear" (1825–1888), Plains Cree, one of the great orators of nineenth-century Canada and a leading theoretician of First Nations rights. Destroyed by the events of 1885. © Library and Archives Canada, 3192491.

letter of the B.C. chiefs to Wilfrid Laurier. I have included it in Other People's Words at the end of the book. You will see that the intellectual line is perfectly consistent.

Of course along the way there have been serious differences of opinion among Aboriginal leaders, just as there are in the House of Commons or between federal and provincial governments. But that has not stopped us working out how to provide good education at all levels, clean water, good health care, road systems, community centres, sports facilities for the non-Aboriginal population. The Honour of the Crown is at stake. It is a matter of the public good. And we have funded all of this, whatever it costs. It is an invaluable investment in our civilization, in our citizenship.

So differences of opinion among Aboriginal leaders is not a valid excuse for the long-standing failures of the Canadian governments. I repeat: the central indigenous messages and demands have long been consistent and clear.

Indigenous leaders have tended not to seek an adversarial relationship. Over time they have sought how to blend their ways with those of the newcomers in order to produce systems that would work. However, through our imported obsession with adversarial approaches to the law and to power, we have forced them onto the legal winners-and-losers path in the twentieth century. The outcome nonetheless favours their consistency and clarity. The courts seem to agree with their point of view. This, in turn, means that we must all come to terms with the central role of the treaties, and for one simple reason: the creation of modern Canada is in good part the outcome of these treaty relationships.

There is an even more basic message in these court victories. They tell us that there is a large, highly sophisticated indigenous leadership. They have thought through their positions.

And they have thought them through with a far clearer and far more consistent sense of Canada's historic commitments than our own governments have. Our governments have persisted in wasting our money by attempting to rewrite history – that is, by denying our treaty and other obligations.

The point is simple. We are living through yet another failure of leadership among our political and administrative leaders. And we are still not judging them and punishing them for their failure on this most important of issues.

On the Aboriginal side, the frustrations are reaching dangerous levels. More than a century has gone by. The same arguments continue. Our leaders either deny the situation or prevaricate or offer piecemeal, patronizing help. And with the Supreme Court's Haida decision on the duty to consult, it is clear that our leaders should be sitting down in an open, transparent way to play their role in charting the road forward.

It does seem that the current prime minister is emotionally unable to engage in open, transparent conversations about these issues. He seems able to function only in private, highly controlled circumstances, followed by eerily controlled public fiats. Sometimes this works. But Canada is a messy confederation that can advance only by embracing its complexity and contradictions in an open and messy way.

Comforting though it may be, it is not enough to blame one leader. What I am describing on these pages is a broad and long-term failure of Canada's leaders. All of them, of all sorts, over an extended period of time.

The indigenous people of Canada now have a large and powerful leadership overflowing with a naturally wide variety of strategies. The more the Canadian leaders refuse to engage, the more fractious the indigenous leaders will become. Why wouldn't they? Why shouldn't they? If positive outcomes are not made possible through open and full consultation by those who lead our governments, well then, anything can happen. And although our leaders will do everything they can to shift the blame, the responsibility will lie with the Government of Canada in all its political and administrative forms.

# XVIII

# THE GREAT ISSUE OF OUR TIME

Leaders are always surprised when the sweep of history intervenes. They have become used to exercising power, setting policy, shaping the public atmosphere, managing the details. Then suddenly their brilliant inevitabilities resemble plasterboard constructions. They collapse or are swept away. Reality reasserts itself. If these people in power are not completely cut off from the world outside their personal domains, they will realize that leaders are rarely remembered as they wish. They get caught in an undertow or crushed in a tsunami. Somehow history, with its use of the collective unconscious, forms the way a government or a prime minister will be remembered.

Most daily dramas slowly disappear from our memories. The details of particular financial policies. Battles to balance budgets. Glorious trade deals. The mishandling of military equipment purchases. Corruption. Senatorial fools. PMO manipulations. Ministerial messes. These triumphs and catastrophes are reduced to the crumbs of the past.

What remains is the public good. Leaders and governments are largely remembered for improving that public good or for worsening it, for great good or great evil. History is pretty unforgiving that way. The leaders' economic theories or social theories – what they think will happen if they do something – don't really count in the long run. What counts over time is what actually did happen.

In other words, governments are not remembered for their day-to-day economic management. That is taken for granted as a basic qualification for governance. Governments are remembered for what they do to better or worsen the shared public good. If Mr. Harper's government, for example, insists that its principal quality has been economic management, then it will damage its own reputation.

After all, it inherited, upon coming to power, a relatively healthy economy with a large surplus. That surplus had been accomplished by Canadians at great cost to ourselves. Through the 1990s, we had accepted a decade of cuts to necessary programs. The new Harper government immediately set about eliminating the surplus through tax cuts. The ministers had been warned by senior finance officials that there was a high risk of some sort of financial crisis. Central bankers around the world were counselling caution.

And yet a government describing itself as led by economists expert in economic management threw away our hard-earned surplus. They threw away our safety margin. The crisis then struck. So the government led us into debt, intentionally or unintentionally. It then devoted the rest of its time in power to getting us out of the debt it had created through bad financial management, while continuing to repeat that theirs was a government led by economists and good financial managers. The war against debt, of course, involved more cuts to programming.

If I were in their shoes, I would not have insisted so

much that their badge of honour was financial management. History is likely to remember them as Canada's worst economic managers since the 1930s. Good management, after all, is about understanding reality and dealing with it. Good economic management is about protecting surpluses, not throwing them away, particularly in risky times, particularly when the resulting deficit doesn't serve a new or improved purpose or build a program that will strengthen society. What we have been living with is a perfectly avoidable deficit brought on by naïveté or incompetence.

Governments are judged above all on what they have done for the public good, unless they have failed as economic managers. In which case they are judged on both.

---

Robert Borden, prime minister during the First World War, was well-intentioned and worked hard, but his reputation has never quite recovered. Why? Because there is a sense that he left behind too many dead and the country deeply divided. John Diefenbaker's reputation, on the other hand, is continually growing because, even if he wasn't a particularly competent government manager, there is a sense that his Prairie radicalism was centred on ideas of egalitarianism and inclusion – ideas that fit with the history of Canada, and helped Canada along that road. His failures as an administrative leader are overwhelmed by the way in which he opened the country up to its real pattern of justice and inclusion, a pattern that draws citizens together. People still talk about the way he and Pandit Jawaharlal Nehru stood together at the 1961 Commonwealth Conference against Britain – and indeed the British monarchy – to keep South

Africa out. This Diefenbaker–Nehru alliance in effect created the modern anti-apartheid movement. There you have the complexity of history. The man who thought he revered Britain will be remembered for having humiliated it and the monarchy in the Commonwealth. History will hold on to that, as it will hold on to his decision to return the vote to Aboriginal people, as well as to remove many of the remaining racist elements in our immigration system. And it was Diefenbaker who laid the foundation for the Charter of Rights, which Pierre Trudeau eventually put in place. And so Diefenbaker will be part of the humanist history of Canada, along with his predecessor and his successor, Louis St. Laurent and Lester Pearson. Despite St. Laurent's embarrassing ending and Pearson's messy governance, all three advanced our sense of the egalitarian and inclusive.

———

History has placed Mr. Harper at the centre of a great Canadian issue: justice for Aboriginal peoples. It is an issue that will help shape who we are, how we see ourselves, how others will see us.

This is the great issue of our time. Why? First, because it is the great outstanding issue of fundamental injustice in Canada, one with a long and destructive history. Chief Justice Beverley McLachlin spoke of this in May 2014. She said she saw the focus of the Court shifting over the next few years from Charter issues to Aboriginal issues. "We're in the early days of the saga." "Canada, I believe, is a project of recon-ciliation. Our successes have always been in recognizing the differences and accommodating them and in working together with respect." And this is the most important issue of reconciliation on our plate. It is a matter of justice and dignity.

The Aboriginal opportunity today is the equivalent of the Quebec issue in the 1960s and 70s. As with the francophones of that era, so the Aboriginals today are ready for a struggle to right the wrongs. And a growing number of non-Aboriginal Canadians are with them.

Yes, there are particular utilitarian issues to be handled. There are economic programs to be launched on reserves, regionally, and nationally. There are hundreds of issues and programs to be worked out. But this is not simply a utilitarian or economic crisis. As David Arnot, chief commissioner for the Saskatchewan Human Rights Commission, has put it, "[T]reaty dialogue did not focus on barter, but on accommodation and trust." What we are faced with is a fundamental social and cultural issue that is of equal importance for all of us, whether Aboriginal or not. It is a question of broad justice. Of fairness. Of social balance. First Nations leaders constantly refer to the treaties as the key to the whole situation because the treaties contain the elements of this fair relationship.

So far Mr. Harper has taken one important step – the apology that was made in the House of Commons in 2008 – and made a few careful moves. For example, the government has named someone in the Privy Council as the prime minister's point person on Aboriginal questions. There have been a few other highly specific initiatives. But the omnibus bills still stand, throwing dark shadows over the Aboriginal role in Canada. And if the analysis of the indigenous leaders is correct, then these omnibus bills represent a dangerous direct attack on Aboriginal rights. History will see them as a symbol of Canada's failure to address the great issue of our time.

# XIX

# EASY THINGS TO DO

It would be so much easier to advance if we could accept that much of the foundation of what we do here comes from here and was agreed upon here. In good part the problem lies in the culture of the Department of Indian Affairs and the lawyers over at Justice. So why not simply remove Indian Affairs and their friends in the Justice Department from anything to do with treaty negotiations?

Why not decide that we don't want haggling as our national policy? Instead, we agree to approach treaty settlements as a way to transfer capital and power – as Quebec did in two northern settlements. Why not create a temporary independent tribunal with the power to settle? It would function as a royal commission except with the power to financially commit the country, the outcomes to be confirmed by Parliament. The fundamental instruction to this body would be that the answer lies in openness to new models, to concepts that respect the understanding of the original agreements. Experimentation with standard law, with financial openness, and with the transfer of wealth and authority might be necessary, if required. Give this body three years to negotiate. Ask a retired Supreme Court justice and a retired national chief to chair it. After all, the justices have been central to historic judgments on Aboriginal questions. They know the subject better than almost anyone. And the choice among the former national chiefs is remarkable: Georges Erasmus, Ovide Mercredi, Phil Fontaine, to name only three. Add perhaps Jean Charest, who negotiated the most recent deal for northern Quebec; former Indian Affairs minister David Crombie; perhaps Sheila Fraser, the last auditor general. Add two senior Aboriginal lawyers with experience in the field.

If the willpower to get on with it were there, the process would not be so difficult – provided two central issues are clear. First, that we do wish to settle. Second, that the intent is to transfer fundamental amounts of power and money, which are important elements of restitution. In that case, the outcome would be a different Canada. Why? Because the critical differences with indigenous people would have been largely addressed.

This sounds so simple. And yet our authorities have spent years not dealing with the epidemic of murders of indigenous women. How then could they deal with treaties? The answer is simple. I repeat this because it must be repeated until it happens. Citizens must recognize the choices and make resolute decisions. The fundamental issues are treaties, power and capital. Are we able to be honest enough with ourselves to accept this? Do we want a settlement or not? The shape and direction of the country depends on how we act. This must become a political issue.

––––––

On a more utilitarian level, why not create an engineering consultancy firm specializing in water, sewage and energy systems for isolated communities? The federal government – not the department – could play the role of convenor and initial funder, holding part of the shares. Aboriginal-owned corporations, like Makivik in Nunavik, could invest as shareholders. It would be important to ensure that a majority of the individual active partners and shareholders – the engineers and other specialists – are Aboriginal. And then, instead of the wasteful, largely ad hoc approach of Indian Affairs, which lurches from one water crisis to another sewage disaster, establish a systematic program to attack the disgraceful lack of infrastructure.

By engaging a critical mass of engineers and other specialists, it would be possible to create new models designed for these conditions. We might at last move away from the old, expensive, polluting system of shipping fuel oil to isolated communities by barge or ice roads.

Again, we have examples that work. We have elements from wind, solar, local hydro and waste-burning energy systems. This is a matter of applied research serving an integrated strategy. And yet we have no systematic approach for assessing communities in order to establish which elements or combination of elements work.

What does a systematic approach mean? Well, I remember arriving in a medium-sized northern town. It was surprising and encouraging to see a big contemporary windmill there, capable of producing much of the town's energy needs. Apparently, local leaders along with a few forward-looking people in the provincial hydro corporation had gotten the windmill built.

But it was immobile. Why? The culture of big hydro in Canada is based on big engineering solutions. The corporation couldn't be bothered keeping the windmill in working order. They wanted to build an energy transmission line, many hundreds of kilometres long, through difficult country, at great expense, with a serious loss of energy per kilometre. This is what real men do. They do big things. In the meantime, the town had to go on shipping in fuel oil.

That is why a large engineering consulting group, with a research and creative capacity, could create new, not-southern, not-urban, not-dense-population points of view and theories of action. There is no reason why Canada should not be a world leader in this area of services for isolated communities. There is even money to be made. And there is a leadership role for Aboriginals. This arrangement would mean moving the money out of Indian Affairs and into an independent, Aboriginal-led program organized to remove the third-world conditions from much of Canadian territory.

———

Housing, housing, housing. One crisis after another. I have seen a lot of those houses. They are sometimes better than they used to be. But even then they are usually southern suburban models minimally adapted for very different conditions. Many are no more than wood rectangles that wouldn't pass for starter cottages. And where is the idea of community in the planning? What are the sources of the contracts and contractors that produce these buildings? What I hear again and again is that the central problem lies with the impenetrable bureaucracy of Indian Affairs and its long established "culture" of treating reserves as temporary internment camps.

Is anyone developing models that have something to do with the place? Yes, here and there. But not often.

Let me give a small example of the problem. In a northern town I was given a tour of three generations of housing for Aboriginals.

The first were shacks, with a few tiny windows. The second were straight out of working-class suburbs in southern Canada: adequate small houses, but inappropriate in shape and in almost every detail for the north, and almost reckless in concept for small isolated communities turned toward nature. The third had some of the details right: a place to store a snowmobile, good insulation. But the architecture still stood out like a foreign infection. The materials showed no local consideration. The living space told you nothing about how people might like to live there. One small detail: to save energy over the long winter, most windows could not be opened, which is very unhealthy in a crowded house. As for the few that did open – and here is a revealing detail – they used a southern wind-out system that would snap the first or second time it was used in severe winter conditions.

What these sorts of details tell us – and there are thousands of other examples – is that no broad effort has been made to think about modern living in isolated and more northerly communities. Modern living that is meshed with indigenous culture and northern isolated communities. This is not a problem. It is a wonderful civilizational challenge. Instead, the few stories of good initiatives are treated more as happy local accidents than as precedents and indicators for further action.

There are architects in all three territories trying their best. There are good buildings here and there – a cultural training centre, for example, on the east coast of Baffin Island – that demonstrate what is possible and appropriate. In the near north, at Laurentian University in Sudbury, a new architectural school is devoted to the idea of living in the north and in isolated communities. This could be seen in the same light as the medical school created early in this century at Laurentian University and at Lakehead in Thunder Bay to focus on health in isolated northern communities. So a few things are happening, but not fast enough. Inefficient funding is another obstacle. Look at the tiny budget for the northern medical school. If we are serious, we should be doubling or tripling it. But above all, the methods of Indian Affairs stand in the way of policy.

One of the most exciting breakthroughs in architecture came in 2014 in Venice, with a major show, called Arctic Adaptations, that involved all twenty-five Nunavut communities and featured suggestions about how to build in the Arctic. At the same time, in *The Walrus*, John van Nostrand laid out an approach to planning and architecture in the middle north.

Perhaps the next step would be to create a national architectural-engineering-building cooperative group specializing in isolated communities. Again, there are many indigenous engineers and architects to take up the leadership role. Include Laurentian, Lakehead and the University of Northern British Columbia in Prince George along with other groups thinking about this. There are elders who have valuable ideas on the relationship between families and place, who think about shapes, materials and colours.

Part of the organization could be focused on identifying and developing the principles, the aesthetics and the needs of architecture, engineering and building in these northern, isolated conditions.

In other words, stop building modified versions of southern bungalows. Stop thinking about living in the north and in isolated communities as an unfortunate accident or a punishment or a failure; stop thinking about it in southern urban terms. Start thinking about it as a purpose in and of itself, a necessary and happy purpose covering two-thirds of Canada, with its own reality.

In the case of both services and housing, a great deal of money is already being spent by the Department. But most of it is spent in an ad hoc, de-intellectualized way, with no sense of broad purpose or initiative. The result is a sort of shapeless defeatism. Turn this into purposeful, integrated initiatives and the same money may produce very different results in both infrastructure and indigenous leadership.

And related to both services and housing, why not immediately strike a group, perhaps chaired by Siila Watt-Cloutier

Siila Watt-Cloutier, Inuk from Nunavik, environmental leader and former International Chair for the Inuit Circumpolar Council. © The Pierce Studio, Brunswick, Maine.

and Georges Erasmus, to start serious public discussions on the creation of a northern university, with a deadline to have it up and running within five years? Yes, we now have universities in Prince George, the Lakehead, Sudbury and Chicoutimi. All of that is in the near north, not even the mid-north. That only leaves half of Canada with nothing. And I do mean a university, with multiple campuses – an intellectual centre for the north. Not just an extension of the northern colleges, not just a training centre to service mining companies. A northern university needs to be a place where northerners can think about themselves in northern terms, where young northerners can gather around intellectual and imaginative leaders.

———

What about creating a co-op banking/microfinance system for the northern two-thirds of Canada? I mean something far more proactive than the largely deposit-banking functions of the existing northern co-op systems. Desjardins and the Vancouver Credit Union both have successful programs aimed at small, isolated communities. It is a question of going a step further to a proactive credit-union approach based entirely on small, isolated communities and devoted to small investment loans.

———

Create and fund – yes, properly fund – a program to help strengthen the more than fifty Canadian languages, more than forty of which are now under threat. This is an emergency.

Languages are disappearing around the world at an unprecedented rate. This represents a loss of complexity and understanding, and Canada is one of the worst examples. There is virtually no federal support for maintaining these languages.

I would ask a simple question of anyone who reads this. Do you want to carry the responsibility – you and your generation – for having overseen the disappearance of forty to forty-five languages indigenous to the place we call Canada? Do you want to be responsible for such a loss of culture, of understanding, of words reaching deep into where we all live? To be complicit in the disappearance of languages, and a good part of their cultures with them, is to be responsible for encouraging a new kind of ignorance.

There is a great deal more to ignorance than the lack of management methods or scientific research. The evils of ignorance come first from not understanding where you are or what that means.

French and English are languages we have taken from elsewhere and partially adapted to our local use. We have been pretty successful at making them local. But what about these more than fifty languages that come from here? That *are* of here? You could say that they are the Canadian languages, languages that have emerged from this place. Languages are deeply unconscious expressions of place – of geography and climate. Of the type of land: arid, mountainous, rivers and lakes. People develop their cultures through their experiences of these places. You have only to look at the effect of large cities on language over the last hundred years to understand this.

And so the indigenous languages of this place do belong to the people through whom they emerged. But they also carry within them an understanding of where we are and what is required of us all. Each time one of these languages disappears, even if you have never heard it, a great steel door closes forever on an understanding of this place. The primary tragedy is for the people who have lost their language, but we have all lost something essential.

This is first a matter of transferring wealth – transferring the money necessary for indigenous peoples to build up their languages. But it is also a matter of focus in our universities. A northern university could join the universities of the near north in reaffirming and building up these languages and cultures. And I do not mean academics getting hold of dying languages in order to make careers out of recording them before the last speakers die, and then living off the corpse. Nor do I mean defending languages as if it were a last-ditch stand. What is needed is stabilization and growth.

There needs to be a national emergency program – involving provincial and territorial ministries of education, but led by indigenous intellectuals and elders – to restructure school and university curricula. Part of this has to do with teaching these languages and cultures and helping in their presentation within the communities concerned. These languages are in danger not because of Darwinian determinism. They have declined because of concrete Canadian policies aimed at destroying them. The undermining of culture and languages on reserves has been partly responsible for today's educational and social difficulties.

There is another big element in this situation. We need to ensure that these languages and cultures become part of mainstream education for all students, as is slowly happening with Cree in Saskatchewan. The rising voice of Aboriginal philosophers like Taiaiake Alfred, Richard Atleo and Leroy Little Bear are also part of this, as is the growing influence of Aboriginal writers. This situation is not easy, precisely because there are so many languages. This isn't like New Zealand with the national role of the Māori. There is no national solution or, in most cases, even a provincial solution. What there can be is a basic principle that indigenous languages and cultures need both a financial transfer to the peoples concerned and the backing of our education systems. Each can be supported to find its place locally or regionally. This is central to the dignity owed to indigenous peoples by all of us. It is part of recognizing their essential contributions in the past, but also recognizing that these languages and cultures have a great deal to contribute to our future. It is part of recognizing that half of the Aboriginal peoples live in cities with other Canadians, and that these languages can grow in our cities. All of this is related to our need to escape the dominance of European-based theories, which are simply not working in our part of the world.

Think about the environmental crisis and our failure to find the language and the theories to deal with it. On the surface, this is a political failure. But more profoundly it is a failure of language and culture, a conceptual failure, a failure of imagination. We are too dependent on intellectual approaches that are not appropriate to our experience – approaches developed for different purposes in a different place.

This is not the first time we have been faced with such a fundamental problem. Until the late nineteenth century, Canadian painters – who create our images of ourselves – were blocked by our reliance on Western European concepts of colour, shape, movement and, perhaps most important, control over movement. We were dependent on a visual sense – an artistic conceit – that still sees humans in control of nature, humans dominant over place. The essential message was that of human civilization as something that defines success as becoming sedentary. Fixed in place. The very concept of *movement stopped* was somehow seen as both a guarantee of perpetuity and an idea of beauty. So much of European art – crowd scenes, portraits, scenes of nature – is conceived as *nature morte*. Perspective, not disorder. Place as background.

The breakthrough of our artists to a violent, uncontrollable idea of colour, of shape, of movement was central to people imagining themselves in a civilization where place was uncontrollable. Where nature was disorder. I wrote about this in *Reflections of a Siamese Twin*.

What I am saying here about language is not related to romanticism or guilt. And it is certainly not related to the interest of academics in becoming the Draculas of dying languages. The seeming indifference of Canadian society to these more than fifty Canadian languages is another leftover of the cultural ideas imported from a sedentary, monolithic tradition that has always feared any internal minority languages as a threat.

I am not suggesting that this is the time for non-Aboriginals to be pontificating about how to save Aboriginal languages or cultures. We have played a large enough role in trying to destroy them. The first thing we need to do is get out of the way, and part of this involves ensuring that systems and budgets favour those languages and cultures.

There is one very practical contribution we can make. Over the last half century Canada has become a world leader in the support and teaching of minority languages, French in particular. We developed French immersion, which often functions in communities where no French is spoken as a first language. A half century ago, almost no anglophone Canadians were bilingual. Now they represent half the bilingual people in the country. Our education systems for small, isolated francophone communities are also remarkable.

In other words, we have proved that language development in difficult conditions is doable. And we know how to do it. So we should know how to be supportive of Aboriginal efforts.

———

Finally, there is the embarrassment of federal underfunding of indigenous education. It simply has to stop. Here is one of the most humiliating failures of our will to act as citizens with a parallel sense of responsibility and empathy.

What of the First Nations education bill that rose and fell in 2014? The more you read Bill C-33, the more contradictory it becomes. Above all, you sense the refusal of the Department of Indian Affairs to let go. The bill begins on an optimistic note. Its purpose is "to enable First Nations control of elementary and secondary education and to provide for related funding."

But reading closer, you see that the new governing body – the Joint Council of Education Professionals – is mentioned only twenty-one times when it comes to the functioning of the system. The minister – that is to say, the civil servants of the department – is mentioned thirty-eight times. The council seems to be above all an advisory body between the department and the First Nations. It has to be consulted, but its power is vague. It is mainly mentioned as an arbiter. The ministerial mentions are all about power. Even the appointment of members to the council leaves it very unclear as to whether First Nations members would have a majority. Above all, the department seems in control of every detail, if it so wishes.

The council is intended to meet only three or four times a year. So it is not even a school board. It is an advisory council. The minister is the voice of authority – that is, the same old bureaucracy.

The bill sets out a clear and absolute obligation to teach English or French. On the other hand, yes, there is a mention of money for First Nations languages, but the conditions as to how this might happen are confusing, to put it politely.

All the mentions of teacher qualifications and graduation measurements come back to provincial standards, meaning provincial controls under the existing non-Aboriginal concept of education. Yes, the bill talks of indigenous culture and languages. But the measurement and enforcement mechanisms are those of the department and the provincial ministries of education.

The former national chief, Shawn A-in-chut Atleo, fought very hard for the money and the program, as did other chiefs. He got both, which was a remarkable breakthrough. But the department held on to its power. And if it gave up anything fundamental, it was to the provincial ministries, not to the First Nations. The bill is another example of the federal government trying to escape its treaty responsibilities by downloading power to the provinces.

And so everything must begin again. Yet, the fundamental bad faith lies in the department. As for the government, it simply isn't clear what they are after.

This could be fixed easily. It is a simple matter of political priorities. Again, citizens could decide to vote for or
against political parties that are willing or unwilling to fund
Aboriginal education at the same level as non-Aboriginal
education, while transferring power to a free-standing, First
Nations–led authority.

———

Six simple ideas. Am I saying that this is a program that will fix
the situation? Not at all. That is not my place. These are merely
illustrations of how negative, pessimistic, ad hoc approaches
to Aboriginal questions can easily be converted into creative,
integrated solutions. And each of these ideas has been raised
by Aboriginal leaders at different times.

What I am saying is that the two departments principally
responsible for indigenous matters continue to act in a deeply
disturbing manner. It is particularly disturbing because, once
the positive, friendly phrases are peeled back, their initiatives
reveal a continuation of the old attitudes toward power and
toward what constitutes an acceptable cultural approach.
They are certainly not at the level of political originality that
permitted so many breakthroughs in Canada in so many other
areas in the past.

At the same time there seems to be little fresh thinking
coming out of any of the other political parties. There are a
few MPs who concentrate on the issue. But no party seems
to have digested the full reality of the Aboriginal comeback.
None has rethought its priorities so that it can act on the
great issue of our time. Nor has any party risen above the
utilitarian mediocrity that now passes for political thought

in our country in order to offer a different approach. On many subjects, Macdonald and Cartier did. As did Laurier. Even Mackenzie King. Diefenbaker. Pearson. Trudeau. Now we seem caught in a bookkeeper mentality, with apologies to bookkeepers.

The road to original thought in political leadership in Canada today leads through the Aboriginal issue. Address that and we will have reimagined how we can function as a civilization. Public systems in Canada have to move out of the controlling, haggling, negative culture attached to the Department of Indian Affairs and its legal appendages. And we as a people need to move from a southern, essentially colonial, extractive-industries point of view to one that looks at the northern two-thirds of Canada and its more or less isolated communities as a purpose and a way of life in and of itself. What we see as impossible difficulties are the result of the country's not investing in broad, thoughtful programs. Many of the solutions lie within the Aboriginal community. And at a minimum we have a fundamental obligation to give support.

# XX

# CHOICE

Choice does exist. Somehow today we don't believe this. It is a phenomenon throughout the West. But in this country such timidity, such fear of creative action, is particularly strange.

We have never been so rich, at least not our society as a whole. We have never been so educated. As individuals we have never done such a wide variety of things: from the old trapping, chopping and digging to technology in outer space and Nobel-worthy writing. And yet we have never been so afraid, as a society, to take broad, imaginative actions of the sort that got us this far.

It is precisely that sort of decisive action, call it societal engagement, that is now needed to embrace with the Aboriginal reality.

What stops us – what stops you – from voting people out of Parliament, out of office, because of their refusal to act on indigenous matters? What stops us – you – from voting people into Parliament, into office, because they have a fair and urgent commitment on indigenous questions at the top of their action plan?

I can think of three barriers.

---

First there is an international, or rather Western, problem. For forty years the standard public discourse shaping responsible leadership has been that choice is limited. Extremely limited. Why? Corporate taxes are bad. Debt is bad. Public initiatives are costly and fail. The market must be left to its own devices. Meanwhile, relax. Enrich yourself. Great economic forces will set the agenda. And if they fail, well, that is the fault of the public good. In any case, there is no other choice.

This has been the central narrative for several generations now. We have been free to manoeuvre carefully within these great truths. And so we work to reduce public debt. Or are made to feel guilty if we don't. Or are punished for not doing so by the international bodies organized to defend the current ideology. Meanwhile our laws are increasingly designed to reward self-interest at the expense of the public good.

Of course it is not true that our choices are limited. There have never been so many possibilities. Think about it: we put public education in place and built our railways long ago, with scarcely any revenues or infrastructure. Why then do we believe today that our options are so limited? Because we have accepted an ideological argument. Some political parties actively advance this ideology. The other parties are too conformist, frightened or unimaginative to change the direction. So when they come to power they limit themselves to fiddling with details.

The core of this ideology is the marginalization of the public good in favour of Hobbesian self-interest: fear the other, look after yourself. More punishment, more prison, more individualism without rules to ensure fairness. Canadians have never really bought into this elite consensus. We have stubbornly held on to the main institutions of the public good, even as the elites chip away at them. They can only chip and try to bury time bombs in vast pieces of legislation, because they know we will vote against anything overt.

But our resistance has been just that: citizen resistance. This is careful citizen wisdom manoeuvring against the massive forces of ideological and administrative conformity. The outcome is obvious: gradually the people wear down. The structures of the public good become fragile, brittle. What else should we expect to happen in the absence of imaginative initiatives and creative reforms?

Instead, in the name of reform, we have had long-term, institutionalized austerity. A cut here. A removal of coverage there. A continual push to do less with less.

But our structures were invented with imagination and purpose. They can be strengthened only if they are reformed with a constant reimagining of the public good from an ethical point of view. Properly enriched, they can even do more with less. That is the creative circle.

Fear of our imagination and the replacement of social purpose with technical efficiency leads to aridity. In the process we become increasingly frightened. As if in a vicious circle, less investment leads to fewer services, leads to a sense that we can't afford what we have, and so on.

As for the mainstream leadership, it has become increasingly confused by the failure of its truths to produce growth or broadly shared prosperity. Unable to admit failure, it has slipped into another kind of fear, one that paralyzes all powers of self-criticism and becomes ever more insistent on continuity. So hand in hand, we and they together grow ever more afraid.

Why is this a barrier to the Aboriginal comeback? Because this generalized sense of threat, this evaporation of the self-confidence necessary for choice and action, undermines our ability to embrace any strategic question and to see it as an opportunity for changing direction in a way that will alter society.

———

The second barrier?

Those institutions of failure that control Aboriginal affairs in Canada have deep roots, and those individuals who have the power to improve things – the ministers, civil servants, Justice Ministry lawyers, political parties, many academics, commentators – can't see themselves as part of the problem.

Very few of them are re-examining the narrative. Their narrative. They are convinced that they are acting in the best interest of those who they believe cannot act for themselves. And, of course, of the taxpayer. But if they were indeed acting in our shared best interest – all of us, Aboriginal and not – how could half the water systems in indigenous communities be below Canadian standards, if not outright tainted? How could they remain that way?

This deformed idea of acting responsibly could almost be described as delusional. And yet these are good people. Or could be good people within a different narrative. Meanwhile their anxiety grows as they find themselves increasingly out of step with their "clients." Perhaps that is why the lawyers from Justice are so aggressive.

In any case, they are moving as if at war with this new and ever larger Aboriginal elite, with the indigenous court victories, with the sustained and broadening narrative coming from indigenous writers, public figures, movements and a growing number of non-Aboriginal supporters. As the cohesion and volume of this narrative grows, so will the incapacity of the official institutions to respond with openness and generosity of spirit only heighten the tension.

What makes this tension increasingly unbearable is that change is coming. They cannot stop it. The Canadian narrative will come to reflect the central indigenous role. The only question is in what conditions.

———

Third, and most important, I am not at all convinced that our society has changed what it believes about the Aboriginal place in Canada. We want to believe we have changed. But look in the mirror. Look at yourself. Ourselves. We have a fundamental and unacceptable situation. Unacceptable social conditions. The founding pillar of our civilization is alienated. Fundamental legal rights are not only denied but opposed by the state. And you and I, we allow all of this to drag on.

Has there been no fundamental change in attitudes? Are we incapacitated by a racism so deeply ingrained that we don't recognize it in ourselves? Does the destructive influence of the extraction industries lie so deep within our governmental systems that we cannot even identify how it cripples our ability to set policies? Or is it an even more profound fear that if those in power were to embrace justice for indigenous peoples the whole narrative that allows them to get up in the

morning and function would collapse? That the whole narrative of European civilization enlightening the northern half of
the continent would evaporate? That the very explanations for
each step taken would become confused? That the legitimacy
of the land-holding system would evaporate?

This third barrier I am describing is about the roots of
authority. It is about the fundamental mythologies that
deliver legitimacy. Ah well, you think, if it is only a matter
of mythology! But if it were *only mythology* why would power
everywhere be so linked to myth? For that matter, why are
writers the only social group still imprisoned and even killed
by the hundreds each year around the world?

Because myth sets the form of power. It gives the force of
legitimacy that allows a society to function. E. Richard Atleo
(Umeek): "[M]yths are a reflection of, and a source of wisdom
about, the nature of reality."

Whether it is racism, deep-set corruption or dependency
on a false myth, the problem remains the same. We have not
made the fundamental decision to change what we believe
about ourselves and our society. We need to take that step in
order to put ourselves in sync with who we really are.

———

How do we take these barriers down?

We might begin by being consistent about the past. We
have agreed that laws matter. Must be obeyed. That the
constitutional division of powers matter. These hundred-
and-fifty-year-old rules define how the federal and provincial
governments function. Basic property laws are centuries old.
We follow them. Our current court system was formalized

by LaFontaine and Baldwin between 1848 and 1851. To the extent that laws are no longer perceived to serve justice, we reform them. But we respect continuity, the reality of the past.

The Supreme Court has made a series of rulings in the last thirty years confirming the Aboriginal position, rights and powers. Why do we allow our governments to ignore these rulings, even though they carry the answers to much of what doesn't work for Aboriginals? Even though they confirm the reality of the indigenous position?

We cannot function as a society if we pick and choose which bits of justice to accept from our past. This is not justice. Nor does it reflect our reality. So we have an obligation – each of us – to make this clear. To ourselves. To those in power.

There is a basic principle in the relationship between indigenous peoples and newcomers going back to 1600. "[I]n the native political and legal system the concept and practice of reciprocity is of fundamental importance." The whole practice, as the Western historian Jean Friesen puts it, of "exchange" had "magical, social, religious, political, individual and moral aspects." "Mutual obligation." "Balanced reciprocity."

Balance and reciprocity. Much of what works in our society is based on balance and reciprocity. Transfer payments. Health care. The only group not to benefit is the group that actually installed this concept of governance. Again, for each of us as citizens it is a matter of being honest with ourselves. We must act to ensure that balance and reciprocity are applied in indigenous relations, as agreed to in the treaties.

This won't happen as long as the Department of Indian Affairs exists, certainly in its current form. The department needs to be stripped of its "ward of the state" powers. As for the lawyers at the Department of Justice, the simple solution to removing the adversarial, verging on violent, atmosphere would be to transfer them elsewhere and bring in lawyers experienced in reconciliation and mediation. There is no lack of lawyers in Canada today who understand treaty questions, understand the need to settle fast, and are sympathetic to the ideas of restitution, reconciliation, balance and reciprocity.

To put this bluntly, the federal and provincial governments and their lawyers seem determined to pretend that repeated rulings of the Supreme Court have not happened. But lots of other lawyers respect the Court and understand these rulings.

———

Stripping the department of its power and changing the legal outline of government is merely a first step. It makes action possible. That action requires massive and urgent consultation – the kind of consultation that does not begin from some corporate decision to dig a hole or build a pipeline.

Yet the government itself admits that it has no "consistent consultation protocol or policy to provide guidance to provinces and companies concerning the level of consultation and forms of accommodation required by the constitutional duty to consult." Why? Because the federal government does not itself have a proper protocol or policy. James Anaya, reporting on the indigenous situation in Canada for the UN Human Rights Council in 2014, pointed out, "[T]he Government appears to view the overall interests of Canadians as adverse to aboriginal interests, rather than encompassing them."

Yet the urgency of the situation calls for an all-encompassing approach. Think of how we turned the situation of francophones and the French language around in the 1960s and 1970s with multiple strategies – financial transfers, francophone minority school boards, French immersion, bilingual government services, public policies on hiring and language skills. We took risks. We invented brand-new approaches. We invested a lot of money. The result has been a remarkable success. Think of how we energized and balanced our immigration/citizenship policies with the point system, myriad support programs, language courses, partnership programs. Again: risk taking, inventions, investment. The result is a cutting-edge approach to citizenship.

In these two areas we understood that we were faced with choosing to act or suffering some very real consequences. So we took action. The effect has been remarkable.

———

The Aboriginal situation is both more fundamental to the country and reflects a more basic social crisis. In 1988 in Edmonton, Georges Erasmus was elected to a second term as national chief. In his acceptance speech he warned: "Canada, if you do not deal with this generation of leaders and seek peaceful solutions, then we cannot promise that you are going to like the kind of violent political action that we can just about guarantee the next generation is going to bring to you." This was not long before Oka.

Asked by a CBC journalist what he meant, Erasmus replied, "We come from a tradition of people where we warn our enemies. Normally we give three warnings. The First Nations have given Canada the first warning." Erasmus wasn't calling for violence any more than Taiaiake Alfred is today. And we

Private Patrick Cloutier, the 22e Régiment, and Brad Larocque, Mohawk Warrior and University of Saskatchewan economics student, during the Oka crisis, September 1, 1990. © Shaney Komulainen/The Canadian Press.

are now well past the third warning. His point was simple: "The Canadian government is not taking our issues seriously." There will be consequences. They still aren't, even though the direction of events is clear. And the consequences are becoming ever more obvious.

———

If you focus on our governments you may become depressed about what is happening. I prefer to focus on the growing power of the indigenous peoples and the existing power that all of us have as citizens.

"Canada is a test case for a grand notion – the notion that dissimilar peoples can share land, resources, power and dreams while respecting and sustaining their differences." So began the commissioners' introduction to the four-thousand-page report of the Royal Commission on Aboriginal Peoples, co-chaired by Georges Erasmus and René Dussault. There it is. There is the narrative that reflects us. "The story of Canada is the story of many such peoples, trying and failing and trying again to live together in peace and harmony."

"But there can be no peace or harmony unless there is justice."

You see here the clarity of an argument that makes sense in the Canadian context. Ovide Mercredi, another remarkable former national chief: "These two goals of remaining distinct peoples and belonging as equals to a larger national community, such as a country, are not inconceivable dreams." Or E. Richard Atleo (Umeek), who writes about how to promote "balance and harmony between beings" using "the laws of the positive side of polarity."

Those among us who are addicted to the Euro-U.S. model of the nation state are confused by such words. They always have been. This is not the logic of the monolithic state with its assertion of a dominant culture and a centralized mythology. In their terms this cannot be a real state. Here lies the core of all negative tensions in Canada. Many of our leaders are themselves addicted to the Euro-U.S. Westphalian model. They desperately attempt to fabricate simplistic myths – peopled by royal families, military triumphs, heroes, Canadian values or Quebec values – that turn out to be lifted directly from Britain or France or the United States. You might say these are simple, old-fashioned concepts of patriotism. But in this case *old-fashioned* refers to a model that has never worked here, a model that leads to the kind of patriotic misery experienced in Europe and the United States when races are ranked, languages forbidden, cultures excluded, one religion set in place as the official faith, or all religions marginalized so that the state's monolithic mythology can become the state religion. This is disingenuously called a secular state. And all of this is done in the name of a safe, aggressively simplified and centralized mythology.

But if that is so, you ask, what is it that holds us together in our non-monolithic model? Go back to the ideas I have been relaying – peace and harmony, balance and harmony, balance and reciprocity. Listen to the elegance of the word *notion* used where others would have needed *nation:* "The notion that dissimilar peoples can share land, resources, power and dreams while respecting and sustaining their differences." "There can be no peace and harmony unless there is justice." This reminds me of the old Canadian motto of *Peace, Welfare and Good Government*, in which *welfare* refers to the public good or justice. I describe this in *A Fair Country.*

Here is one more quote. Alexander Morris, lieutenant governor of Manitoba in the 1870s and chief treaty negotiator: "[I wish] to take the Ojibwa by the hand and never let go your hand." We know that his motives were mixed, even confused. But we also know that these words were "accepted and understood in a moral as well as literal sense." And he knew this himself. That's why he used the words. He wished them to be understood that way. He committed the state to a permanent reciprocal relationship. It hardly matters what the legal papers say because in an oral relationship the legal relationship *is* oral. That is why the Supreme Court so often decides for the Aboriginal side.

A court of justice cannot reward hypocrisy or outright lies. The government and its representatives repeatedly constructed Canada by using the language and meaning of Aboriginal peoples – the language of long-term commitments in the most complete sense. As the strength of indigenous peoples returns, the courts are holding our governments to the language they used in order to gain power.

That is good for all of us, and for a very good reason. To the extent that Canada was built through the use of Aboriginal concepts, the door is open to all of us imagining ourselves in a way that is both interesting and appropriate. And the growing Aboriginal leadership has already made an invaluable contribution. It has given itself the skills necessary to understand not only the indigenous points of view but also the cultural confusion of the rest of us. This matters because we have not yet learned to listen. I think this is why so many indigenous intellectuals are making the effort not only to explain themselves, but to describe how they see the system.

Jim Dumont: "The prevailing and dominating worldview that surrounds us today and to which we are compelled to respond is one that is narrow in its vision, exclusive and detached in relating to the total environment, analytical and deductive in its perception and thinking, linear in its doing, and hierarchical and competitive in its management of the field of activity." In other words, it is "deficient in most of the qualities of higher intelligence."

But wait, the crisis is in the Aboriginal world. Is it not? Yes, there are unresolved indigenous problems, many of them the outcome of policies and structures maintained by Canada.

But is the more profound crisis not in the non-Aboriginal world? If not, why would we find it so difficult to listen – to listen seriously – to the points of view coming from the founding pillar of our civilization? Are we so insecure? So frightened to absorb views that after all have been central to Canada's establishment and survival? Or is it a lack of sensibility? An emotional wall constructed unconsciously to protect ourselves from the reality of this place? Or a simple lack of consciousness? Or all of the above?

Leroy Little Bear: "Any individual within a culture is going to have his or her own personal interpretation of the collective cultural code; however the individual's world view has its roots in the culture – that is, in the society's shared philosophy, values and customs. If we are to understand how Aboriginal and Eurocentric world views clash, we need to understand how the philosophy, values and customs of Aboriginal culture differ from those of Eurocentric cultures."

I began *A Fair Country* by saying that Canada is a métis civilization, a civilization influenced by the Métis model of complexity. The Métis people have demonstrated that complexity can be a civilizational model. Their power and influence through the eighteenth and nineteenth centuries and their role as political and economic intermediaries are an illustration of this. Look at how important they were in shaping the fur trade, making possible what the Europeans called exploration and negotiating relationships, including treaties. We non-Aboriginals are somehow a disordered version of their formalized complexity. Leroy Little Bear argues that the last hundred and fifty years have undone, but not destroyed, separate existences, and have left Aboriginal peoples with "a heritage of jagged worldviews." "[A] random puzzle, a jigsaw puzzle." You could say the same of non-Aboriginals. The difference is that indigenous peoples have a conscious sense of this complexity. "Aboriginal consciousness became a site of overlapping, contentious, fragmented, competing desires and values." The challenge today is how to use this complexity. As the indigenous elite grows stronger, its members are drawing from this overlapping fragmentation the very different roots and shapes of their own origins. How? By using their "ambidextrous consciousness."

Key to this has been the emergence of formalized, written indigenous philosophy, schools of philosophy based in universities. It is a burgeoning world. Things are being said. Philosophers are proposing ethical outlines for society. And their arguments are rooted here. Compare this with the mainstream departments of philosophy, mired as they are in footnoting European ideas, an arid world of colonial references.

Where does all of this leave non-Aboriginals? On the surface we have slowly declined into an unhappy state of self-satisfaction based on utilitarian views of society. Public policy is reduced to self-interest and the mechanics of administration. This satisfies no one, so we must be distracted by wildly improbable attempts at jingoism. And jingoism takes us back to the old European models of belonging.

———

So the philosophical questions are important. How are we to imagine ourselves? The answer shapes what we think we can do.

Jim Dumont: "The circle, then, being primary, influences, in every way, how we see the world. In the process of how life evolves – how the natural world grows and works together, how all things move toward their destiny while changing from one stage to another – the circle should be evidenced everywhere we look."

The idea of conceiving society in this way is no longer a mystery to many Canadians. We have learned something over the last few years. Or remembered. But we seem now to be at the point where some will say – *Ah yes, the circle, of course, of course* – as if to say – *Enough, let's get back to something serious like rational management,* as if already nervous to be on non-linear territory. There is still a strong sense that only the rational, linear approach is properly sophisticated and requires constant attention and study, while the circular, inclusive approach is somehow romantic and simplistic. I could easily argue that the exact opposite is true.

Here we come close to why the Aboriginal comeback is so important for all of us. Look, for example, at Canada's approach to immigration and citizenship. It owes nothing to the Western rational idea of how to organize a nation state or to define belonging. That is why it is successful. It is entirely a product of circular ideas of belonging, the almost unconscious outcome of immigrants being welcomed here in a particular way over three centuries by indigenous peoples. When it goes wrong – the migrant workers program, for example – it is always the result of an attempt to rationalize or Europeanize or Americanize the system.

The risk of veering off track is heightened today by the growing atmosphere of fear in the West, pushed hard by the various security services and the revived old-style national-ists. Those who function through fear cannot help but see the relaxed, open, happily confused Canadian approach to immi-gration and citizenship as a threat. If our system works, well then, their own devotion to fear is suddenly misplaced.

Do they really care? I certainly notice the negative pressure on our approach whenever I am in an international gathering of experts, for example on security or immigration. They seem comfortable talking only about migrants, identity politics, the impossible differences between ethnicities and religions. They don't want to talk about immigrants transforming themselves with relative ease into engaged citizens and working with others in a relaxed way across ethnic and religious differences.

Here you see the power of the indigenous conceptual approach to belonging. Leroy Little Bear: "The function of Aboriginal values and customs is to maintain the relationships that hold creation together." This is the exact opposite of the deconstructive approach dominant in the West.

During the 1960s and 70s a small group of Westerners, including Rachel Carson, Barbara Ward and Maurice Strong, developed environmentalism into an international movement. Phrases like *sustainable development* and *biodiversity* emerged. Maurice Strong's role has been that of organizer across cultural lines, both political and intellectual. He organized the UN's 1972 environmental conference in Stockholm, then the United Nations Environmental Programme, then the 1992 Earth Summit in Rio. He was closely involved with and influenced by indigenous peoples in Canada. This began in 1945, when he left school in southern Manitoba, aged sixteen, to work in the Inuit community of Chesterfield Inlet, now known as Igluligaarjuk, in Nunavut.

Why do I mention this? Because the environmental movement seems now to be held back by Western intellectual structures that have sidelined the major questions, like global warming, into a confusion of competing facts and a desperate attempt to analyze these questions from a linear, utilitarian point of view. Any conceptual or holistic approach is ridiculed or punished. But you can only change directions on major issues through a conceptual, holistic approach. Leroy Little Bear: "All things are animate, imbued with spirit, and in constant motion. In this realm of energy and spirit, interrelationships between all entities are of paramount importance, and space is a more important referent than time."

A few years ago this would have been automatically dismissed as talking to rocks. Now we can see that it is a philosophy that allows biodiversity to make sense, as well as the idea of sustainability. And for that matter the ideas of balance and harmony.

E. Richard Atleo (Umeek) explains that Western ideas of democracy miss a whole series of essential elements present in indigenous philosophy. Why do we have so much trouble taking sustainability seriously? Because our underlying ideas of progress and individual rights eliminate it. Continuity is not a Western democratic idea. But it is an indigenous idea. Atleo: "The democratic principle of continuity, which addresses the fundamental issue of the right of life forms to continue their ways of life, does not formally exist within the constitutions of the Western world."

In other words, the Aboriginal comeback carries with it many ideas and approaches to ideas that represent a great advantage for all of us.

———

On March 8, 2013, for the second time in a young year, the courts spoke out on Aboriginal issues and more specifically on Métis questions. This time it was the Supreme Court, and it settled the question of the rights of the Manitoba Métis to land. Once again the Court came down clearly on their

It had taken almost 150 years, but in 2013 the Supreme Court ruled
in favour of the Manitoba Métis land claim, a quest begun by Louis Riel
(1844–November 16, 1885). © Glenbow Museum, NA-504-3.

side. Since the 1870s the Métis have argued that the federal
government had acted improperly and unfairly toward them.
And now, at last, the Supreme Court has made it perfectly
clear that the Manitoba Métis had been cheated out of their
land by the Government of Canada. That is, by you and me.
That the Government of Canada betrayed the Honour of the
Crown. And we are the Crown. You and I.

So there will be some sort of restitution. This is the inevitable evolution of events. This is where we are going.

But the old question remains. Will we – you and I – once again prevaricate, drag it out, haggle? Will we allow our government and their lawyers – our lawyers – to act this way? Or will we embrace this restitution with enthusiasm as an opportunity to right a wrong and so put our country back on track?

In the same month as this court decision, the federal budget introduced a First Nations Job Fund aimed at youth. There had been no consultations with First Nations. The description of this job training program talked of "mandatory participation," "compliance" and so on. This sounds like very old-fashioned, top-down, authoritarian do-gooding. It doesn't sound like a respectful approach. And it certainly doesn't sound like an appropriate way to treat citizens, particularly given the government's obligation to consult first, as laid out in the Haida court decision. The residential-school movement was filled with language like *mandatory* and *compliance*, all done in the best interest of *those Indians*.

A few months later the First Nations education bill was launched. It eventually produced the resignation of Shawn A-in-chut Atleo as national chief, then ground to a halt.

In the midst of all this confusion of contradictory initiatives, the Truth and Reconciliation Commission came to Vancouver. In the middle of a West Coast downpour, as many as seventy thousand citizens marched through the city in support of the Aboriginal cause.

On June 25, 2014, the City Council of Vancouver voted unanimously to acknowledge that the city sits on unceded Aboriginal territory. This is not merely a politeness or a formality. Yes, it is a gesture of respect to the Musqueam, Squamish and Tsleil-Waututh First Nations. "[T]hese territories were never ceded through treaty, war or surrender," the

Seventy thousand citizens march for reconciliation through a Vancouver downpour, September 22, 2013. © Pauline Petit/Reconciliation Canada.

motion reads. Beyond reconciliation, Vancouver's decision represents the beginning of a form of restitution. The city will adopt "appropriate protocols" for doing business. What does that mean? Well, it could mean the first steps in reconceptualizing the public space so that indigenous ways come back into the core of how we do things and what we do.

A day later, on June 26, the Supreme Court ruled on the case of the Tsilhqot'in Nation versus British Columbia. They ruled that full Aboriginal title to land does exist. This is a dramatic confirmation of the resurgence of Aboriginal power and influence. It confirms the evolution of the last half century, changes the nature of all remaining treaty negotiations and classifies the need for corporations to deal with Aboriginal authorities as if they have authority. It was a historic day for Aboriginal peoples, but also for all of us. It is one of the most important legal decisions of our contemporary era.

British Columbia's minister of justice made an almost positive statement in response: "The decision provides additional certainty around processes and tests that are applied to the relationship between the Province and Aboriginal peoples." The federal minister used the standard avoidance phrase: the government will review the "complex and significant issues" in the decision. But then he tried to drive a wedge between Aboriginals and non-Aboriginals, calling for "settlements that balance the interests of all Canadians." There was no hint of the need to right wrongs. No hint of a right to justice for indigenous peoples. Everything was reduced to a utilitarian argument over interests; that is, self-interest, in which the interests of thirty-two million apparently selfish people are to be weighed against – that is, opposed to – those of less than two million apparently selfish people. This approach is demeaning for all thirty-four million of us. What it means is that the government cannot bring itself to admit what is happening. But it is happening anyway.

In the Tsilhqot'in statement made after the ruling, I noticed these words describing the governmental approach: "[An] impoverished view of title." And those of Grand Chief Phillip of the Union of British Columbia's Indian Chiefs: "The Supreme Court of Canada completely repudiated the greatly impoverished and highly prejudicial position of the B.C. and Federal governments."

Impoverished! I don't want to be part of an ethically, intellectually, culturally impoverished policy. An impoverishment of the Honour of the Crown.

This is a matter of self-respect. But it is also about politics. Taiaiake Alfred: "Politics is the force that channels social, cultural, and economic powers and makes them imminent in our lives. Abstaining from politics is like turning your back on a beast when it is angry and intent on ripping your guts out."

There was a small sign of change during the 2014 Quebec election. In the northern riding of Ungava, Inuit and other Aboriginals made a concerted effort to defeat a party that had always held the seat. The Aboriginals had the potential to hold the balance of power, and they succeeded. At both the federal and provincial levels, this could be true in many non-urban ridings. With half the Aboriginals living in cities, it could also be true for many Western downtown seats. Add to this the possible use of their votes by non-Aboriginals who understand that this is the great issue of our time. All together, these votes could represent the balance of power in Parliament and in many legislatures. It is a matter of making it clear to parties and candidates that this is an issue that will weigh heavily when we vote.

———

There is a great deal of talk today about the importance of authenticity in what people and societies do. More and more of us sense that we must rethink our narrative, re-examine our myths.

What is happening around Aboriginal people today in Canada is all about authenticity. Theirs. Ours. Theirs and ours shared in some way. All of us, from indigenous peoples to the original francophones and anglophones and through the successive waves of immigration to the most recently sworn-in citizen, must examine our actions.

Failure at this time will do more than shape the memory of a government or the reputation of a prime minister. It will affect us all, in the way that the hanging of Louis Riel still affects the reputation of John A. Macdonald and dogs our sense of ourselves as a country.

But if we start down a road of shared reconciliation and restitution, we will have taken a crucial step in building a sense of ourselves and the country. It is a matter of being true to where we are, to what is fair and possible here. That consciousness, that sense of ourselves, will solidify our ability to live together and to do so in an atmosphere of justice.

Jean Teillet

# OTHER PEOPLE'S
# WORDS

Wab Kinew

# 1763

# THE ROYAL PROCLAMATION

*This extract from the Royal Proclamation puts in place
our modern understanding of "Indian rights." Here they
are guaranteed by the newly installed empire, British in
place of French. The protections and engagements are clear.
Of course, the king makes assertions about his power over
lands that he, his armies and his administrators have neither
conquered nor seen. In fact, they would not be capable of
seeing, let alone governing, these lands for at least another
hundred years without the guidance and leadership of the
very "Indians" the king pretends to be protecting. Such is the
conceit of empires. I have put some of the key lines in italics.*

**By the King.**
**A PROCLAMATION.**
**GEORGE R.**

... And whereas it is just and reasonable, and essential to
Our Interest and the Security of Our Colonies, *that the several
Nations or Tribes of Indians, with whom We are connected, and who live
under Our Protection, should not be molested or disturbed in the Possession*

of such Parts of Our Dominions and Territories as, not having been ceded to, or purchased by Us, are reserved to them, or any of them, as their Hunting Grounds; We do therefore, with the Advice of Our Privy Council, declare it to be Our Royal Will and Pleasure, that no Governor or Commander in Chief in any of Our Colonies of Quebec, East Florida, or West Florida, do presume, upon any Pretence whatever, to grant Warrants of Survey, or pass any Patents for Lands beyond the Bounds of their respective Governments, as described in their Commissions; as also, that no Governor or Commander in Chief in any of Our other Colonies or Plantations in America, do presume, for the present, and until Our further Pleasure be known, to grant Warrants of Survey, or pass Patents for any Lands beyond the Heads or Sources of any of the Rivers which fall into the Atlantick Ocean from the West and North-West, or upon any Lands whatever, which, not having been ceded to, or purchased by Us as aforesaid, are reserved to the said Indians, or any of them.

And We do further declare it to be Our Royal Will and Pleasure, for the present as aforesaid, to reserve under Our Sovereignty, Protection, and Dominion, for the Use of the said Indians, all the Lands and Territories not included within the Limits of Our said Three New Governments, or within the Limits of the Territory granted to the Hudson's Bay Company, as also all the Lands and Territories lying to the Westward of the Sources of the Rivers which fall into the Sea from the West and North West, as aforesaid; and We do hereby strictly forbid, on Pain of Our Displeasure, all Our loving Subjects from making any Purchases or Settlements whatever, or taking Possession of any of the Lands above reserved, without Our especial Leave and Licence for that Purpose first obtained.

*And We do further strictly enjoin and require all Persons whatever, who have either wilfully or inadvertently seated themselves upon any Lands within the Countries above described, or upon any other Lands, which, not having been ceded to, or purchased by Us, are still reserved to the said Indians as aforesaid, forthwith to remove themselves from such Settlements.*

*And whereas great Frauds and Abuses have been committed in the purchasing Lands of the Indians, to the great Prejudice of Our Interests, and to the great Dissatisfaction of the said Indians; in order therefore to prevent such Irregularities for the future, and to the End that the Indians may be convinced of Our Justice, and determined Resolution to remove all reasonable Cause of Discontent,* We do, with the Advice of Our Privy Council, strictly enjoin and require, that no private Person do presume to make any Purchase from the said Indians of any Lands reserved to the said Indians, within those Parts of Our Colonies where We have thought proper to allow Settlement; but that if, at any Time, any of the said Indians should be inclined to dispose of the said Lands, that same shall be purchased only for Us, in Our Name, at some publick Meeting or Assembly of the said Indians to be held for that Purpose by the Governor or Commander in Chief of Our Colonies respectively, within which they shall lie: and in case they shall lie within the Limits of any Proprietary Government, they shall be purchased only for the Use and in the Name of such Proprietaries, conformable to such Directions and Instructions as We or they shall think proper to give for that Purpose: And We do, by the Advice of Our Privy Council, declare and enjoin, that the Trade with the said Indians shall be free and open to all our Subjects whatever; provided that every Person, who may incline to trade with the said Indians, do take out a Licence for carrying on such Trade from the Governor or Commander in Chief of any of Our Colonies respectively, where such Person shall reside; and also give Security to observe such Regulations as We shall at any Time think fit, by Ourselves or by Our Commissaries to be appointed for this Purpose, to direct and appoint for the Benefit of the said Trade....

Given at Our Court at *St. James's*, the Seventh Day of October, One thousand and seven hundred and sixty three, in the Third Year of Our Reign.

**GOD SAVE THE KING.**

# THAYENDANEGEA (JOSEPH BRANT) TO SIR FREDERICK HALDIMAND, GOVERNOR OF QUEBEC

## A Letter

*Joseph Brant, the Mohawk leader, had many qualities and therefore a few weaknesses. A master of guerrilla warfare, he was successful against American forces before he moved himself and his people to the Grand River in Canada. The Six Nations are still there. Brant was a great linguist, a charismatic leader and speaker, and a remarkable diplomat. But he also had a powerful sense of the written argument. Here he bawls out the senior European in Canada for not keeping his word. The result was a series of concessions and offers of land in Canada.*

*By the way, Asharekowa means Big Sword or Great Knife; in other words, it is a term of respect for a military*

*leader. Note that in a civilization based on family
relationships, the great soldier Brant addresses the great
soldier and governor Haldimand as Brother. Again, key
lines are put in italics.*

Brother Asharekowa and Representatives of the King, the
sachems and war chieftains of the Six United Nations of
Indians and their allies have heard that the King, their Father,
has made peace with his children, the Americans; and when
they heard of it, they found that they were forgot and no
mention made of them in said Peace, wherefore they have now
sent me to inform themselves before you of the real truth,
whether it is so or not, that they are not partakers of that peace
with the King and the Americans. We were greatly cast down
when we heard that news, and it occasions great discontent
and surprise with our people, wherefore tell us the real truth
from your heart, and we beg that the King will be put in mind
by you and recollect what we have been when his people first
saw us, and what we have since done for him and his subjects.

Brother, We, the Mohawks, were the first Indian Nation that
took you by the hand like friends and brothers, and invited
you to live amongst us, treating you with kindness upon your
debarkation. We were then a great people ... conquering
all Indian nations round about us, and you in a manner but
a handful, after which you increased the degrees and we
continued your friends and allies, joining you from time to
time against your enemies.

*At last we assisted you in conquering all Canada, and for joining you
so firmly and faithfully you renewed your assurances of protecting and*

*defending ourselves, lands and possessions against any encroachment whatsoever,* procuring for us the enjoyment of fair and plentiful trade of your people, and sat contented under the shade of the tree of peace, tasting the favour and friendship *of a great nation bound to us by treaty,* and able to protect us against all the world. Wherefore, *we on our side have maintained an uninterrupted attachment towards you, in confidence and expectation of reciprocity, and to establish a perpetual friendship and alliance between us. We were unalterably determined to stick to our ancient treaties with the Crown of England with the determined resolution inviolably to adhere to our alliance at the risk of our lives,* families and property, the rest of the Six Nations finding the firmness and steadiness of us, the Mohawks, followed our example and espoused the king's cause to the present instant.

Wherefore, Brother, I am now sent in behalf of all the king's Indian allies to receive a decisive answer from you, and to know whether they are included in the treaty with the Americans, as faithful allies should be, or not, and whether those lands which the Great Being above has pointed out from our ancestors, and their descendants, and placed them from the beginning and where the bones of our forefathers are laid, is secure to them, or whether the blood of their grandchildren is to be mingled with their bones, through the means of our allies for whom we have so often freely bled.

*May 21, 1783*

# 1869

# LOUIS RIEL

## DECLARATION
## Of the People of Rupert's Land and the North West

*Yes, Riel was a martyr, ripped apart by the impossibility of
his situation. But he is also officially recognized as the Father
of Manitoba. He was an interesting political thinker who
attempted to weave together the Métis reality with Western
ideas of citizen rights and Catholic conservatism. This was
an impossible combination, but those were the cards fate had
dealt him. At his best he was also a clever political strategist.*

*Here is the declaration of independence that would
eventually produce the province of Manitoba. It is also a first
chess move in a negotiation.*

*Note the Burkean balance of rights and responsibilities;
the use of European/U.S. rights-of-man principles; the
differentiation between commerce and citizenship; the
explanation of the sources of constitutional legitimacy; and
the reminder that the Métis had been the long-term military
defenders of the North-West.*

WHEREAS, it is admitted by all men, as a fundamental principle that the public authority commands the obedience and

respect of its subjects. It is also admitted that a people when it has no Government is free to adopt one form of Government in preference to another to give or to refuse allegiance to that which is proposed. In accordance with the first principle the people of this Country had obeyed and respected that authority to which the circumstances surrounding its infancy compelled it to be subject.

A company of adventurers known as the "Hudson's Bay Company" and invested with certain powers granted by His Majesty (Charles II.) established itself in Rupert's Land, AND IN THE NORTH-WEST TERRITORY for trading purposes only. This Company, consisting of many persons, required a certain constitution. But as there was a question of commerce only, their constitution was framed in reference thereto. Yet, since there was at that time no government to see to the interests of a people already existing in the country, it became necessary for judicial affairs to have recourse to the officers of the Hudson's Bay Company. Thus inaugurated that species of government, which, slightly modified by subsequent circumstances, ruled this country up to a recent date.

WHEREAS, this government thus accepted was far from answering the wants of the people, and became more and more so as the population increased in numbers, and as the country was developed, and commerce extended, until the present day, when it commands a place amongst the Colonies; and this people ever actuated by the above mentioned principles, had generously supported the aforesaid government, and gave to it a faithful allegiance; when, contrary to the law of nations, in March, 1869, that said Government surrendered and transferred to Canada all the rights which it had or pretended to have in this territory, by transactions with which the people were considered unworthy to be made acquainted.

AND WHEREAS, it is also generally admitted that a people is at liberty to establish any form of government it may consider suitable to its wants, as soon as the power to which it was subject abandons it, or attempts to subjugate it without its consent, to a foreign power; and maintain that no right can be transferred to such foreign power. Now, therefore,

1st. We, the Representatives of the people in Council assembled at Upper Fort Garry, on the 24th day of November, 1869, after having invoked the God of nations, relying on these fundamental moral principles, solemnly declare in the name of our constituents and in our own names, before God and man, that from the day on which the Government we had always respected, abandoned us by transferring to a strange power the sacred authority confided to it, the people of Rupert's Land and the North-West became free and exempt from all allegiance to the said Government.

2d. That we refuse to recognize the authority of Canada, which pretends to have a right to coerce us and impose upon us a despotic form of government still more contrary to our rights and interests as British subjects than was that Government to which we had subjected ourselves through necessity up to a recent date.

3rd. That by sending an expedition on the 1st of November charged to drive back Mr. William McDougall and his companions coming in the name of Canada to rule us with the rod of despotism without a previous notification to that effect, we have but acted conformably to that sacred right which commands every citizen to offer energetic opposition to prevent his country being enslaved.

4th. That we continue and shall continue to oppose with all our strength the establishing of the Canadian authority in our country under the announced form. And in case of persistence on the part of the Canadian Government to enforce its obnoxious policy upon us, by force of arms, we protest before hand against such an unjust and unlawful course, and we declare the said Canadian Government responsible before God and men for the innumerable evils which may be caused by so unwarrantable a course.

Be it known, therefore, to the world in general and to the Canadian Government in particular, that as we have always heretofore successfully defended our country in frequent wars with the neighbouring tribes of Indians, who are now on friendly relations with us, we are firmly resolved in future not less than in the past, to repel all invasions from whatsoever quarter they may come.

And furthermore, we do declare and proclaim in the name of the people of Rupert's Land and the North-West that we have on the same 24th day of November, 1869, above mentioned, established a Provisional Government, and hold it to be the only and lawful authority now in existence in Rupert's Land and the North-West, which claim the obedience and respect of the people.

That meanwhile we hold ourselves in readiness to enter into such negotiations with the Canadian Government, which may be favourable for the good government and prosperity of this people.

In support of this declaration, relying on the protection of Divine Providence, we mutually pledge ourselves on oath, our lives, our fortunes, and our sacred honor to each other.

Issued at Fort Garry this 8th day of December in the year of our Lord one thousand eight hundred and sixty-nine.

(Signed,)     JOHN BRUCE, President.
              LOUIS RIEL, Secretary.

# 1884

# ON THE BANNING OF THE POTLATCH

## House of Commons Debate

From 1884 to 1951, the potlatch ceremony, or celebration, was banned by law through an amendment to the Indian Act. The potlatch was a spiritual event as well as an important social moment. It also involved a leader redistributing wealth by lavish gift giving. At first the enforcement of the ban was sporadic. Then, in 1913, the poet Duncan Campbell Scott took over as deputy superintendent general of Indian Affairs. He was determined to enforce the law. The case famous for "killing" the potlatch came early in 1922 in Alert Bay, a Kwakiutl island off the northeast coast of Vancouver Island. Following a large celebration organized by Chief Dan Cranmer, charges were laid. More than fifty people were convicted. More than twenty, including women, spent time in prison. It was a terrible humiliation.

What was it about the potlatch that so upset the government and Parliament? After all, there were no calls to ban European-style celebrations/ceremonies involving, by European work ethic standards, a wasteful spending of money on parties and presents. Weddings and balls thrown by rich Euro-Canadians were admired as rites of success. The bigger the better. And such ostentation had no philosophical or legal purpose. After all, most people were content to be quietly married with a couple of witnesses.

What was it that so upset Canadian leaders? Perhaps it was the possibility of profound meaning attached to a generosity that did not have European roots. After all, this was not Christian charity. No guilt was involved. The proposal of such a different world order couldn't help but disturb the missionaries. And it certainly undermined the authority of the local Indian agents. After all, who were they compared with rich and generous indigenous leaders?

The attacks on the potlatch are particularly noteworthy because they were attempts to humiliate both the indigenous leaders themselves and the indigenous idea of leadership.

I remember sitting in the big, pleasant kitchen of Dan Cranmer's daughter, Gloria Webster, overlooking the ocean off Alert Bay. She was then on the Board of Directors of the Museum of Civilization; her advice was being sought at the national level. Of course the anger was still there. Her father had been jailed for political reasons. But the attempt to break Kwakiutl culture had failed.

There is one detail worth noticing in the parliamentary exchange between the prime minister, John A. Macdonald, and the leader of the Opposition, Edward Blake: the sexual references. There is nothing quite like the erotic fantasies of Victorian gentlemen. Macdonald fulminates against debauchery, orgies and wife swapping. He talks of "a great debauch." If people weren't about to be harmed by the government's actions, it would all be highly comical. That none of it was true is beside the point. As in Victorian novels and travel books, earnest, punishing, repressed Christian

*gentlemen seem to enjoy fantasizing that "savages" lead a*
*free life. There is an element of fantasy voyeurism. There is*
*also a hint here of a late-nineteenth-century euro mindset that*
*could justify the sexual exploitation that lay ahead in the*
*residential schools.*

*This debate in the House of Commons illustrates the*
*fabulist style of racism that led to the potlatch ban.*

### Second Reading, March 24, 1884

Sir JOHN A. MACDONALD. The third clause provides that celebrating the "Potlach" is a misdemeanour. This Indian festival is a debauchery of the worst kind, and the departmental officers and all clergymen unite in affirming that it is absolutely necessary to put this practice down. Last year the late Governor General issued a proclamation on the advice of his Ministers warning Indians against celebrating this festival. At these gatherings they give away their guns and all their property in a species of rivalry, and go so far as to give away their wives; in fact, as I have said, it is a great debauch.

———

### Third Reading, April 7, 1884

Sir JOHN A. MACDONALD. This is a new clause for the purpose of putting down the Indian Festival known as the "potlatch" which is the cause of a great deal of misery and demoralization in British Columbia. The representations made to the Government on this subject, not only by the Indian agent but by the clergy are very strong. They say it is utterly useless, especially on Vancouver Island, where the "potlach" principally exists, to introduce orderly habits while it is in vogue. They meet and carry on a sort of mystery; they remain for weeks, and sometimes months, as long as they can get food, and carry on all kinds of orgies. It is lamentable to read the accounts given by the clergy of British Columbia, and they urge that some legislation on the subject should take place. It was suggested by the clergy there that it would have some effect if the Governor General should issue a proclamation, warning the Indians against this unhappy custom, and though it did have some effect, it was not at all commensurate with the expectations which were founded upon it, and it is proposed to introduce this clause. I have here a number of statements from both the Catholic and the Protestant missionaries, showing the awful effects of this custom, but I need not trouble the House by reading them.

Mr. BLAKE. I think anybody who has read descriptions of this feast will not doubt that it has a very demoralising tendency in a great many ways. I have had accounts of men of apparently very considerable financial and commercial power among the Indians of British Columbia, some of whom I believe have accumulated considerable wealth, and it is all dissipated in the insane exuberance of generosity which seems to be encouraged by these meetings. But the custom is a very old and a very inveterate one amongst them; and without at all saying that the case is not ripe for the passage of such a clause as this, it seems to me that one should be very cautious in attempting suddenly to stop, by the harsh process of the criminal law, the known customs and habits of these tribes. I would therefore strongly recommend the hon. gentleman, with reference to the minimum punishment of two months, to alter the clause, so that for the first two years an almost nominal punishment might, if the authorities thought it expedient, be imposed in the first instance. The point to be attained is to the getting the Indians gradually to see that this practice is contrary to the law; and by the force of the trial and a very trifling punishment the first time, with a warning that would spread amongst them that a much severer punishment might be inflicted on the next occasion, would perhaps repress the practice. But the necessity of inflicting two months' punishment might turn out to be calamitous necessity.

1910

# THE MEMORIAL TO
# SIR WILFRID LAURIER, PREMIER
# OF THE DOMINION OF CANADA

From the Chiefs of the Shuswap, Okanagan and
Couteau Tribes of British Columbia

*Note the subtlety and sophistication of the argument made
by the chiefs. While they seem to be complimenting the
prime minister, they are actually laying out a complete
narrative that clearly states their position and their rights
as the true owners of their land. It is they who have invited
European guests to share their lives. They have some
confidence in Laurier because he is a "real white," that is,
a French Canadian. They came first and acted properly.
A half century later the English Canadians appeared and
acted badly. They are the "other whites." Remember that
the word Father simply means that they are paying him the
compliment of treating him as if he were an elder in their own
family. And so he is a father among many.*

*I have put a few of the lines in italics to highlight the
clarity of their argument, which is sometimes ironic. It is*

*important to follow the full narrative. As you will see, the
chiefs are proposing a balanced and inclusive approach
toward civilization.*

*Perhaps most important, you will find here, laid out in
detail more than a century ago, precisely the arguments put
forward today.*

*The chiefs were Chief John Tetlenitsa from the
Nlaka'pamux Nation, Chief Petit Louis from the Secwépemc
Nation and Chief John Chilahitsa from the Syilx Nation.*

Dear Sir and Father,

We take this opportunity of your visiting Kamloops to speak a
few words to you. We welcome you here, and *we are glad we have
met you in our country.* We want you to be interested in us, and to
understand more fully the conditions under which we live. We
expect much of you as the head of this great Canadian Nation,
and feel confident that you will see that we receive fair and
honorable treatment. Our confidence in you has increased
since we have noted of late the attitude of your government
towards *the Indian rights movement of this country* and we hope that
with your help our wrongs may at last be righted. *We speak to
you the more freely because you are a member of the white race with whom
we first became acquainted,* and which we call in our tongue "real
whites."

One hundred years next year they came amongst us here at
Kamloops and erected a trading post. After the other whites
came to this country in 1858 we differentiated them from the
first whites as their manners were so much different, and we
applied the term "real whites" to the latter (viz., the fur-traders

of the Northwest and Hudson Bay companies. As the great majority of the companies' employees were French speaking, the term latterly became applied by us as a designation for the whole French race). The "real whites" we found were good people. We could depend on their word, and we trusted and respected them. They did not interfere with us nor attempt to break up our tribal organizations, laws, customs. They did not try to force their conceptions of things on us to our harm. Nor did they stop us from catching fish, hunting, etc. They never tried to steal or appropriate our country, nor take our food and life from us. They acknowledged our ownership of the country, and treated our chiefs as men. *They were the first to find us in this country. We never asked them to come here, but nevertheless we treated them kindly and hospitably and helped them all we could. They had made themselves (as it were) our guests.*

*We treated them as such, and then waited to see what they would do.*

*As we found they did us no harm our friendship with them became lasting. Because of this we have a 'warm heart to the French at the present day.' We expect good from Canada.*

When they first came among us there were only Indians here. They found the people of each tribe supreme in their own territory, and having tribal boundaries known and recognized by all. The country of each tribe was just the same as a very large farm or ranch (belonging to all the people of the tribe) from which they gathered their food and clothing, etc., fish which they got in plenty for food, grass and vegetation on which their horses grazed and the game lived, and much of which furnished materials for manufactures, etc., stone which furnished pipes, utensils, and tools, etc., trees which furnished firewood, materials for houses and utensils, plants, roots, seeds, nuts and berries which grew abundantly and were gathered in their season just the same as the crops on a ranch, and used for food; minerals, shells, etc., which were used for ornament and for plants, etc., water which was free to all. Thus, fire, water, food, clothing and all the necessaries of life were obtained in abundance from the lands of each tribe, and all the people had equal rights of access to everything they required. You will see the ranch of each tribe was the same as its life, and without it the people could not have lived.

Just 52 years ago the other whites came to this country. They found us just the same as the first or "real whites" had found us, only we had larger bands of horses, had some cattle, and in many places we cultivated the land. They found us happy, healthy, strong and numerous. Each tribe was still living in its own "house" or in other words on its own "ranch." No one interfered with our rights or disputed our possession of our own "houses" and "ranches," viz., our homes and lives. We were friendly and helped these whites also, for had we not learned the first whites had done us no harm? Only when some of them killed us we revenged on them. Then we thought there are some bad ones among them, but surely on the whole they must be good. Besides they are the queen's people. And we had already heard great things about the queen from the "real whites." We expected her subjects would do us no harm, but rather improve us by giving us knowledge, and enabling us to do some of the wonderful things they could do.... Soon they saw the country was good, and some of them made up their minds, to settle it. They commenced to take up pieces of land here and there. They told us they wanted only the use of these pieces of land for a few years, and then would hand them back to us in an improved condition; meanwhile they would give us some of the products they raised for the loan of our land. *Thus they commenced to enter our "houses," or live on our "ranches." With us when a person enters our house he becomes our guest, and we must treat him hospitably as long as he shows no hostile intentions. At the same time we expect him to return to us equal treatment for what he receives. Some of our Chiefs said, "These people wish to be partners with us in our country. We must, therefore, be the same as brothers to them, and live as one family. We will share equally in everything — half and half — in land, water and timber, etc. What is ours will be theirs, and what is theirs will be ours. We will help each other to be great and good."*

The whites made a government in Victoria — perhaps the queen made it. We have heard it stated both ways. Their chiefs dwelt there. *At this time they did not deny the Indian tribes owned the whole country and everything in it.* They told us we did. We Indians were hopeful. We trusted the whites and waited patiently for their chiefs to declare their intentions toward us and our lands. We knew what had been done in the neighboring states, and we remembered what we had heard about the queen being so good to the Indians and that her laws carried out by her chiefs were always just and better than the American laws. Presently chiefs (government officials, etc.) commenced to visit us, and had talks with some of our chiefs. They told us to have no fear, the queen's laws would prevail in this country, and everything would be well for the Indians here. They said a very large reservation would be staked off for us (southern interior tribes) and the tribal lands outside of this reservation the government would buy from us for white settlement. They let us think this would be done soon, and meanwhile until this reserve was set apart, and our lands settled for, they assured us we would have perfect freedom of traveling and camping and the same liberties as from time immemorial to hunt, fish, graze and gather our food supplies where we desired; also that all trails, land, water, timber, etc., would be as free of access to us as formerly. Our chiefs were agreeable to these propositions, so we waited for these treaties to be made, and everything settled. We had never known white chiefs to break their word so we trusted. In the meanwhile white settlement progressed. Our chiefs held us in check. They said, "Do nothing against the whites. Something we did not understand retards them from keeping their promise. They will do the square thing by us in the end."

What have we received for our good faith, friendliness and patience? Gradually as the whites of this country became more and more powerful, and we less and less powerful, they little by little changed their policy towards us, and commenced to put restrictions on us. Their government or chiefs have taken every advantage of our friendliness, weakness and ignorance to impose on us in every way. They treat us as subjects without any agreement to that effect, and force their laws on us without our consent and irrespective of whether they are good for us or not. They say they have authority over us. They have broken down our old laws and customs (no matter how good) by which we regulated ourselves. They laugh at our chiefs and brush them aside. Minor affairs amongst ourselves, which do not affect them in the least, and which we can easily settle better than they can, they drag into their courts. They enforce their own laws one way for the rich white man, one way for the poor white, and yet another for the Indian. They have knocked down (the same as) the posts of all the Indian tribes. They say there are no lines, except what they make. They have taken possession of all the Indian country and claim it as their own. Just the same as taking the "house" or "ranch" and, therefore, the life of every Indian tribe into their possession. They have never consulted us in any of these matters, nor made any agreement, "nor" signed "any" papers with us. They have stolen our lands and everything on them and continue to use same for their own purposes. They treat us as less than children and allow us 'no say' in anything. They say the Indians know nothing, and own nothing, yet their power and wealth has come from our belongings. The queen's law which we believe guaranteed us our rights, the B.C. government has trampled underfoot. This is how our guests have treated us – the brothers we received hospitably in our house.

After a time when they saw that our patience might get exhausted and that we might cause trouble if we thought all the land was to be occupied by whites they set aside many small reservations for us here and there over the country. This was their proposal not ours, and we never accepted these reservations as settlement for anything, nor did we sign any papers or make any treaties about same. They thought we would be satisfied with this, but we never have been satisfied and never will be until we get our rights. We thought the setting apart of these reservations was the commencement of some scheme they had evolved for our benefit, and that they would now continue until they had more than fulfilled their promises but although we have waited long we have been disappointed. We have always felt the injustice done us, but we did not know how to obtain redress. We knew it was useless to go to war. What could we do? Even your government at Ottawa, into whose charge we have been handed by the B.C. government, gave us no enlightenment. We had no powerful friends.... For a time we did not feel the stealing of our lands, etc., very heavily. As the country was sparsely settled we still had considerable liberty in the way of hunting, fishing, grazing, etc., over by far the most of it. However, owing to increased settlement, etc., in late years this has become changed, and we are being more and more restricted to our reservations which in most places are unfit or inadequate to maintain us. Except we can get fair play we can see we will go to the wall, and most of us be reduced to beggary or to continuous wage slavery. We have also learned lately that the British Columbia government claims absolute ownership of our reservations, which means that we are practically landless. We only have loan of those reserves in life rent, or at the option of the B.C. government. Thus we find ourselves without any real home in this our own country.

In a petition signed by fourteen of our chiefs and sent to your Indian department, July, 1908, we pointed out the disabilities under which we labor owing to the inadequacy of most of our reservations, some having hardly any good land, others no irrigation water, etc., our limitations re pasture lands for stock owing to fencing of so-called government lands by whites; the severe restrictions put on us lately by the government re hunting and fishing; the depletion of salmon by over-fishing of the whites, and other matters affecting us. In many places we are debarred from camping, traveling, gathering roots and obtaining wood and water as heretofore. Our people are fined and imprisoned for breaking the game and fish laws and using the same game and fish which we were told would always be ours for food. Gradually we are becoming regarded as trespassers over a large portion of this our country.... We have no grudge against the white race as a whole nor against the settlers, but we want to have an equal chance with them of making a living. We welcome them to this country. It is not in most cases their fault. They have taken up and improved and paid for their lands in good faith. It is their government which is to blame by heaping up injustice on us. But it is also their duty to see their government does right by us, and gives us a square deal. We condemn the whole policy of the B.C. government towards the Indian tribes of this country as utterly unjust, shameful and blundering in every way. We denounce same as being the main cause of the unsatisfactory condition of Indian affairs in this country and of animosity and friction with the whites. So long as what we consider justice is withheld from us, so long will dissatisfaction and unrest exist among us, and we will continue to struggle to better ourselves. For the accomplishment of this end we and other Indian tribes of this country are now uniting and we ask the help of yourself and government in this fight for our rights. We believe it is not the desire nor policy of your government that these conditions should exist. We demand that our land question be settled, and ask that treaties be made between the government and each of our tribes, in the same manner as accomplished with the Indian tribes of the other provinces of Canada, and in the neighboring parts of the United States. We desire that every matter of importance to each tribe be a subject of treaty, so we may have a definite understanding with the government on all questions of moment between us and them. In a declaration made last month, and signed by twenty-four of our chiefs (a copy of which has been sent to your Indian department) we have stated our position on these matters. Now we sincerely hope you will carefully consider everything we have herewith brought before you and that you will recognize the disadvantages we labor under, and the darkness of the outlook for us if these questions are not speedily settled. Hoping you have had a pleasant sojourn in this country, and wishing you a good journey home, we remain

Yours very sincerely,

The Chiefs of the Shuswap, Okanagan and Couteau
or Thompson tribes
– Per their secretary, J.A. Teit –

*Presented at Kamloops, August 25, 1910*

# AMENDMENTS TO THE INDIAN ACT, 1927

*Here is a clear and intentional act of evil. Here are the things
forbidden to "Indians" by their government, which is to say
our government, between 1927 and 1951, which includes
a ban on the hiring of lawyers. This is an attempt to break
the new political form of the Indian Rights Movement. You
have to imagine that this horrible text was written by your
grandfather or great-grandfather. It was certainly written by
one of our grandfathers, corrected by another one, approved
by an assistant deputy minister and a deputy minister, both
great-grandfathers of someone out there. Finally, hundreds
of our grandfathers passed this amendment to the Indian Act
through the House of Commons and the Senate. And then
hundreds more of our grandfathers enforced the law, going
home in the evening to sing hymns, say grace at the table
and play with their children. That would be our parents or
grandparents.*

Section 140

    (1) Every Indian or other person who engages in, or assists
    in celebrating or encourages either directly or indirectly

another to celebrate any Indian festival, dance or other ceremony of which the giving away or paying or giving back of money, goods or articles of any sort forms a part, or is a feature, whether such gifts of money, goods or articles takes place before, at, or after the celebration of the same, or who engages or assists in any celebration or dance of which the wounding or mutilation of the dead or living body of any human being or animal forms a part or is a feature, is guilty of an offence and is liable on summary conviction to imprisonment for a term not exceeding six months and not less than two months.

(2) Nothing in this section shall be construed to prevent the holding of any agricultural show or exhibition or the giving of prizes for exhibits there at.

(3) Any Indian in the province of Manitoba, Saskatchewan, Alberta, or British Columbia, or in the Territories who participates in any Indian dance outside the bounds of his own reserve, or who participates in any show, exhibition, performance, stampede, or pageant in aboriginal costume without the consent of the Superintendent General or his authorized agent, and any person who induces or employs any Indian to take part in such dance, show, exhibition, performance, stampede or pageant, or induces any Indian to leave his reserve or employs any Indian for such a purpose, whether the dance, show, exhibition, stampede or pageant has taken place or not, shall on summary conviction be liable to a penalty not exceeding twenty-five dollars, or to imprisonment for one month, or to both penalty and imprisonment.

———

Section 141

Every person who, without the consent of the Superintendent General expressed in writing, receives, obtains, solicits, or requests from an Indian any payment or contribution for the purpose of raising a fund or providing money for the prosecution of any claim which the tribe or band of Indians to which such Indian belongs, or of which he is a member, has or is represented to have for the recovery of any claim or money for the benefit of the said tribe or band, shall be guilty of an offence and liable upon summary conviction for each such offence to a penalty not exceeding two hundred dollars and not less than fifty dollars or to imprisonment for a term not exceeding two months.

# 1971

# GRAND CHIEF DAVID COURCHENE

**Foreword to *Wahbung: Our Tomorrows***

*Wahbung was the answer of the Manitoba Indian
Brotherhood through its grand chief to the Trudeau
government's 1969 White Paper (Statement of the
Government of Canada on Indian Policy), the last open
attempt by a Canadian government to propose assimilation
of the Aboriginal peoples. Grand Chief Courchene states
the Aboriginals' case with an eloquent directness that
demonstrates how the Canadian narrative needed to be
profoundly altered. Some of this has now been done —
the enshrining of Aboriginal rights in the 1982 revised
Constitution, for example. But we all know that the
fundamental change has not yet come.*

**Message of the Grand Chief**

We, the first people of this land now called Manitoba, are a
people of indomitable will to survive, to survive as a people,
strong and creative.

During the centuries in which we lived on this land, we faced many times of struggle, for the land is not always kind, and our people like any other people had to find ways to adapt to a changing environment.

These last one hundred years have been the time of most difficult struggle, but they have not broken our spirit nor altered our love for this land nor our attachment and commitment to it. We have survived as a people.

Our attachment means that we must also commit ourselves to help develop healthy societies for all the peoples who live upon this land. But we will not be able to contribute unless we have the means first to develop a healthy society for ourselves. Since the signing of the Treaties one hundred years ago, we have been constantly and consistently prevented from doing so.

Three fundamental facts underlie this paper and are reflected in all aspects of it.

First, we are determined to remain a strong and a proud and identifiable group of people.

Second, we refuse to have our lives directed by others who do not and who can not know our ways.

Third, we are a 20th-century people, not a colorful folkloric remnant. We are capable and competent and perfectly able to assess today's conditions and develop ways of adjusting positively and successfully to them.

Other Canadians must recognize these three facts.

We ask you for assistance for the good of all Canada and as a moral obligation resulting from injustice in the past, but such assistance must be based upon this understanding. If this can be done, we shall continue to commit ourselves to a spirit of cooperation.

Only thus can hope be bright that there might come a tomorrow when you, the descendants of the settlers of our lands, can say to the world, Look, we came and were welcomed, and then we wrought much despair; but we are also men of honour and integrity and we set to work in cooperation, we listened and we learned, we gave our support, and today we live in harmony with the first people of this land who now call us, brothers.

We hope that tomorrow will come.

# 1977

# GRAND CHIEF JOHN KELLY

We Are All in the Ojibway Circle
Kenora, Ontario
Testimony before the Royal Commission on the Northern
Environment

*Here we are, 194 years after Joseph Brant's letter to
Haldimand and 67 years after the British Columbia chiefs'
letter to Laurier, and yet another indigenous leader, John
Kelly, finds it necessary, yet again, to lay out the history, the
agreements broken, the possibility of a healthy relationship.
Over the intervening years, all across the country,
commissioners had appeared in community after community
and pushed hard for treaties. Intentionally or unintentionally,
they misrepresented the contents of those treaties. And then the
treaties were not fulfilled.*

*Hundreds, probably thousands, of other Aboriginal
leaders have spoken up over the years, each in their own
way. The drawers and filing cabinets of the Department
of Indian Affairs must be jammed full of such carefully
reasoned representations. Each time one of these came in, the
Canadian strategy has been to make a note to file, then to
put the file away and lock the drawer. Either that or send*

*it over to the lawyers at Justice to start a protracted court battle.*

*What strikes me first is the patience of people like Chief Kelly. Once again, yet again, all over again, he explains the obligations and responsibilities, ethical, social and legal, of Canadians and of our governments. What is beginning to change by the late 1970s is not the attitude of indigenous peoples. They have stayed on track. But now the federal and provincial governments have started to realize — oh so slowly — that this is a situation that will not go away.*

*You can find the full text of Grand Chief Kelly's testimony in the anthology* From Ink Lake, *edited by Michael Ondaatje.*

Mr. Commissioner, welcome to the territory of Treaty No. 3. It has been a long time since a Commission came to this region. The last time was in the early 1870s. In 1873, those long-ago proceedings gave us Treaty No. 3 – a treaty that has never been kept.

Now, one hundred and four years later, we are visited by another Commission – a Royal Commission on the Northern Environment. I sincerely wish we could whole-heartedly applaud your activity. I genuinely would like to talk of happy things. I would love to be able to rejoice in great achievements and plan for greater successes in the future. Unfortunately, that is not yet possible. Time, history and the white man have made it so.

But we have learned from the past. We have been made wary of Commissions that show promise. Due to our bitter history my people feel we must be cautious about unreservedly endorsing your inquiry. Until we see the way in which your Commission is conducted, we must be hesitant in giving you our unqualified support.

Allow me to explain…. The way the present situation has come about is something like this. An Indian was sitting on a log feeling very comfortable because he had all the room he needed. A white man came along and said that he had been running a long time and was terribly tired. The bishop's men wanted to burn him alive and the king's soldiers were chasing him with guns. Could he please have a little place on the log so that he might rest from his awful journey. The Indian willingly shared a piece of his log with the white man. But the white man felt like stretching himself and asked for a little more room. The Indian let him have a little more of his log. The white traveller was satisfied for a short while but then he felt he wanted some more space. The Indian gave it to him. Of course, the guest did not go hungry or cold. Like a decent host, the Indian shared his pemmican and furs with the poor, harassed foreigner. As the time passed, it just so happened that the stock of food and clothing came under the control of the white man; the Indian was cold and hungry and barely holding on to the end of the log. Now the white man did not at all fancy the idea of sharing his log with such a miserable and sickly creature. It deeply hurt his sense of property. So he told the Indian to get off the log, but in his vast charity he suggested that the Indian could sit on a stump further away in the bush. Since 1871, the Ojibway of north-western Ontario have been sitting on the stump. In the last few years, we have begun to panic because the white man on the log is casting his eyes on our stump. Granted, the stump is small and damn prickly but at least we have a place to sit and occasionally we have been able to grab a bit of the game and cast the line for a fish.

These are the results of the last Commission which was sent to this part of the country. Our land and resources were stolen. You, Mr Commissioner, have a golden opportunity to recommend that some of what is ours must be returned.

The first Commission travelled here and convinced my forefathers to sign a treaty. At that time our government needed our land as a passageway to the prairies for troops to fight the *métis*. It was also needed as a route for the settlers and, most of all, for its rich natural resources. My people were not informed of the reasons why you wanted a treaty, and you did not give us an opportunity to research and determine exactly what was in our best interests. My forefathers signed the treaty. They were deceived about its contents. They were never told about its effect. They were convinced they had no choice but to sign. And, with trust in the good faith and intentions of the Treaty Commission, my forefathers signed the treaty in 1873.

Our research tells us that the early Treaty Commissioners indeed had good faith and intentions. Nevertheless, history must judge them as unwilling pawns in a process aimed at destroying the native people. We warn you, Mr Commissioner, to be wary of becoming another well-intentioned pawn – and an unwitting tool of rich and powerful interests. Many well-intentioned people come before me and before the Band Chiefs of Treaty No. 3 all the time. But it is your duty to look behind the good intentions and understand the long historical process of which we are all merely a part.

Let me tell you what happened to us after the Treaty Commissioners went back to the government carrying the Xs of my forefathers on a treaty that my ancestors didn't understand.

The Commissioners reported that they had secured a surrender of all Ojibway rights in the Treaty No. 3 area. They explained that, in return for that surrender, the government was basically happy. It was pleased to have the land surrender. Land was all they wanted. However, the government was not pleased with the treaty promises and consequently only made half-hearted efforts to implement them.

In the meantime, the Ojibway Chiefs returned to their bands. The Chiefs reported they had agreed with the representatives of the benevolent white queen that the Ojibway people should not prevent the white man's access to, and passage over, Treaty No. 3 land. The Chiefs reported that the government's representative had said the traditional Ojibway life would not be disturbed. The Chiefs told of the promises made by the white negotiators. From then on, the Ojibway ceased all resistance to white intrusion and were prepared to share their land with the white man. We knew we had given up much by allowing the white man to enter Ojibway territory and we, therefore, looked forward to receiving the benefits and guarantees promised by the Treaty Commissioners.

Briefly, let me tell you what happened. If the Treaty Commissioners could be here to listen to the outcome of their well-intentioned efforts they might feel as saddened and betrayed as we do.

Not long after the treaty was made, a dispute arose between the Federal government and the Provincial government as to which government had jurisdiction over the Treaty No. 3 territory. Ontario said its western borders included Treaty No. 3. Ottawa said no. Ottawa claimed Ontario did not extend as far west as Treaty No. 3. Do not forget, Mr Commissioner, that at that time there was still no so-called development here. While the governments were arguing about lines on a map, my people continued to go about their business of living comfortably and securely from the riches of the land.

The dispute between the governments was not settled until the question was put before the highest court of the time. That court ruled, in 1888, that Ontario's western boundary did include most of the Treaty No. 3 territory. We are told that the legal consequence of this decision (which we did not know had been rendered) was that the surrender of our land (which we did not know had taken place) was not to the government which we had been dealing with, but to a government in a place called Toronto. That was a government we had never met with nor had any particular desire to meet. We didn't know what was going on because no one informed us. And no one provided us with the resources needed in order to inform ourselves. We only found out there was something drastically wrong when we became aware that the promises made to us by the Treaty Commissioners were largely unfulfilled.

―――――

We were not consulted, or even advised that this was happening. While the Federal government stood by, we were knowingly robbed by the Ontario government. We shall never forget it. Neither shall we rest until we get back what is ours.

―――――

By dwelling on the early years following the signing of the Treaty, I do not wish to suggest that our grievances all occurred many years ago. On the contrary. Despite being robbed time and again by the government, and more recently by industry, we still possess certain things of value which the white man covets. We have learned through our experience that wherever Indians possess or control anything economically valuable, there will always be those who will attempt to steal it. But, worst of all, your society and the government which appointed you seem to encourage, or at least condone, the theft of Indian lands. Apparently Indian lands are fair game while white lands are protected by very strict laws.

Almost always what is stolen from us is what you call natural resources. We propose to itemize and particularize our concerns in relation to national resources.

———

Mr Commissioner, it seems to me that the stranger from the sunrise beyond the lakes just keeps coming back. Each time he promises us perpetual repose and gluttony, and leaves us with famine and disease. It also appears that, as the years go by, the circle of the Ojibway gets bigger and bigger. Canadians of all colours and religion are entering that circle. You might feel that you have roots somewhere else, but in reality, you are right here with us. I do not know if you feel the throbbing of the land in your chest, and if you feel the bear is your brother with a spirit purer and stronger than yours, or if the elk is on a higher level of life than is man. You may not share the spiritual anguish as I see the earth ravaged by the stranger, but you can no longer escape my fate as the soil turns barren and the rivers poison. Much against my will, and probably yours, time and circumstance have put us together in the same circle. And so I come not to plead with you to save me from the monstrous stranger of capitalist greed and technology. I come to inform you that my danger is your danger too. My genocide is your genocide.

To commit genocide it is not necessary to build camps and ovens. All that is required is to remove the basis for a way of life.

# A WORD FROM COMMISSIONERS

## The Royal Commission on Aboriginal Peoples

*The importance of this Commission cannot be overstated. Led
by former national chief Georges Erasmus and Justice René
Dussault, their hearings and report rewrote or re-established
the original Canadian narrative. Unfortunately, the
government decided to ignore its recommendations.*

*But the work was done. The history laid out. The
possibilities explained. And despite the resistance of a
succession of federal and provincial governments, this
narrative is slowly making its way into the mainstream. Here
is an extract from the eloquent introduction to the final four-
thousand-page report.*

Canada is a test case for a grand notion – the notion that
dissimilar peoples can share lands, resources, power and
dreams while respecting and sustaining their differences.
The story of Canada is the story of many such peoples,
trying and failing and trying again, to live together in peace
and harmony.

But there cannot be peace or harmony unless there is justice.

We began our work at a difficult time.

- It was a time of anger and upheaval. The country's leaders were arguing about the place of Aboriginal people in the constitution. First Nations were blockading roads and rail lines in Ontario and British Columbia. Innu families were encamped in protest of military installations in Labrador. A year earlier, armed conflict between Aboriginal and non-Aboriginal forces at Kanesatake (Oka) had tarnished Canada's reputation abroad and in the minds of many citizens.

- It was a time of concern and distress. Media reports had given Canadians new reasons to be disturbed about the facts of life in many Aboriginal communities: high rates of poverty, ill health, family break-down and suicide. Children and youth were most at risk.

- It was also a time of hope. Aboriginal people were rebuilding their ancient ties to one another and searching their cultural heritage for the roots of their identity and the inspiration to solve community problems.

We directed our consultations to one over-riding question: *What are the foundations of a fair and honourable relationship between the Aboriginal and non-Aboriginal people of Canada?*

Successive governments have tried – sometimes intentionally, sometimes in ignorance – to absorb Aboriginal people into

Canadian society, thus eliminating them as distinct peoples. Policies pursued over the decades have undermined – and almost erased – Aboriginal cultures and identities.

This is assimilation. It is a denial of the principles of peace, harmony and justice for which this country stands – and it has failed. Aboriginal peoples remain proudly different.

Assimilation policies failed because Aboriginal people have the secret of cultural survival. They have an enduring sense of themselves as peoples with a unique heritage and the right to cultural continuity.

This is what drives them when they blockade roads, protest at military bases and occupy sacred grounds. This is why they resist pressure to merge into Euro-Canadian society – a form of cultural suicide urged upon them in the name of 'equality' and 'modernization.'

Assimilation policies have done great damage, leaving a legacy of brokenness affecting Aboriginal individuals, families and communities. The damage has been equally serious to the spirit of Canada – the spirit of generosity and mutual accommodation in which Canadians take pride.

Yet the damage is not beyond repair. The key is to reverse the assumptions of assimilation that still shape and constrain Aboriginal life chances – despite some worthy reforms in the administration of Aboriginal affairs.

To bring about this fundamental change, Canadians need to understand that *Aboriginal peoples are nations*. That is, they are political and cultural groups with values and life ways distinct from those of other Canadians. They lived as nations – highly centralized, loosely federated, or small and clan-based – for thousands of years before the arrival of Europeans. As nations, they forged trade and military alliances among themselves and with the new arrivals. To this day, Aboriginal people's sense of confidence and well-being as individuals remains tied to the strength of their nations. Only as members of restored nations can they reach their potential in the twenty-first century.

Let us be clear, however. To say that Aboriginal peoples are nations is not to say that they are nation-states seeking independence from Canada. They are collectivities with a long shared history, a right to govern themselves and, in general, a strong desire to do so in partnership with Canada.

―――

We hope that our report will also be a guide to the many ways Aboriginal and non-Aboriginal people can begin – right now – to repair the damage to the relationship and enter the next millennium on a new footing of mutual recognition and respect, sharing and responsibility.

# 2000

# LEROY LITTLE BEAR

## Jagged Worldviews Colliding

*There has been a rapid growth not in Aboriginal philosophy,*
*but in Aboriginals who give their philosophy a written*
*form that competes on shared intellectual ground with the*
*Western model. Leroy Little Bear is a Blood of the Blackfoot*
*Confederacy. He is also the doyen of these thinkers. He*
*is from southern Alberta and is a senior professor at the*
*University of Lethbridge. He is always clear, and gives*
*meaning to the word wise. What follows are the fragments of*
*an argument that we should all read in full.*

Any individual within a culture is going to have his or her
own personal interpretation of the collective cultural code;
however, the individual's worldview has its roots in the
culture – that is, in the society's shared philosophy, values,
and customs. If we are to understand why Aboriginal and
Eurocentric worldviews clash, we need to understand how the
philosophy, values, and customs of Aboriginal cultures differ
from those of Eurocentric cultures.

In Aboriginal philosophy, existence consists of energy. All things are animate, imbued with spirit, and in constant motion. In this realm of energy and spirit, interrelationships between all entities are of paramount importance, and space is a more important referent than time. Although I am referring to the philosophy of the Plains Indians, there is enough similarity among North American Indian philosophies to apply the concepts generally, even though there may be individual differences or differing emphases.

The idea of all things being in constant motion or flux leads to a holistic and cyclical view of the world. If everything is constantly moving and changing, then one has to look at the whole to begin to see patterns. For instance, the cosmic cycles are in constant motion, but they have regular patterns that result in recurrences such as the seasons of the year, the migration of the animals, renewal ceremonies, songs and stories. Constant motion, as manifested in cyclical or repetitive patterns, emphasizes the process as opposed to product. It results in a concept of time that is dynamic but without motion. Time is part of the constant flux but goes nowhere. Time just is.

———

All the above leads one to articulate Aboriginal philosophy as being holistic and cyclical or repetitive, generalist, process-oriented, and firmly grounded in a particular place.

———

The function of Aboriginal values and customs is to maintain the relationships that hold creation together. If creation manifests itself in terms of cyclical patterns and repetitions, then the maintenance and renewal of those patterns is all-important. Values and customs are the participatory part that Aboriginal people play in the maintenance of creation.

———

In contrast to Aboriginal value systems, one can summarize the value systems of Western Europeans as being linear and singular, static, and objective. The Western European concept of time is a good example of linearity. Time begins somewhere way back there and follows a linear progression from A to B to C to D. The linearity manifests itself in terms of social organization that is hierarchical in terms of both structure and power. Socially, it manifests itself in terms of bigger, higher, newer, or faster being preferred over smaller, lower, older, or slower.

Singularity manifests itself in the thinking process of Western Europeans in concepts such as one true god, one true answer, and one right way. This singularity results in a social structure consisting of specialists. Everyone in society has to be some kind of specialist, whether it be doctor, lawyer, plumber, or mechanic. Specializations are ranked in terms of prestige. This, in turn, results in a social class structure. Some professions are higher up the ladder, and some are lower down it. In sciences, singularity manifests itself in terms of an expensive search for the ultimate truth, the ultimate particle out of which all matter is made. And so it goes.

―――――

Colonization created a fragmentary worldview among Aboriginal peoples. By force, terror, and educational policy, it attempted to destroy the Aboriginal worldview – but failed. Instead, colonization left a heritage of jagged worldviews among Indigenous peoples. They no longer had an Aboriginal worldview, nor did they adopt a Eurocentric worldview. Their consciousness became a random puzzle, a jigsaw puzzle that each person has to attempt to understand. Many collective views of the world competed for control of their behaviour, and since none was dominant, modern Aboriginal people had to make guesses or choices about everything. Aboriginal consciousness became a site of overlapping, contentious, fragmented, competing desire and values.

―――――

Yet all colonial people, both the colonizer and the colonized, have shared or collective views of the world embedded in their languages, stories, or narratives. It is collective because it is shared among a family or group. However, this shared worldview is always contested, and this paradox is part of what it means to be colonized. Everyone attempts to understand these different ways of viewing the world and to make choices about how to live his or her life. No one has a pure worldview that is 100 percent Indigenous or Eurocentric; rather, everyone has an integrated mind, a fluxing and ambidextrous consciousness, a precolonized consciousness that flows into a colonized consciousness and back again. It is this clash of worldviews that is at the heart of many current difficulties with effective means of social control in postcolonial North America. It is also this clash that suppresses diversity in choices and denies Aboriginal people harmony in their daily lives.

# CHIEF JOSEPH GOSNELL OF THE NISGA'A

### Speaking at Harvard

*It took twenty-five years of negotiation before the Nisga'a people got a treaty they felt they could accept. The government of Canada wasted our money and the Nisga'a leadership's time. A whole generation had to be given over to bringing our government to an arrangement that Ottawa could have easily accepted after one or two years.*

*Chief Gosnell is an imposing figure. He conveys ethical clarity in a restrained way that I can only describe as toughness combined with nobility. He dealt with Canadian officials from a great height, radiating what the British would call "noblesse oblige." Here is a prime minister we could perhaps have had, if our small minds in the Department of Indian Affairs had not forced him to devote his whole life to treaty negotiations. What is striking is the grace and humour with which he carried this burden of endless negotiation. You will get a sense of this in his Harvard speech.*

The Nisga'a people have long sought to negotiate our way *into* Canada – to become full participants in the social, political, and economic life of our country. Our treaty makes this possible. Following more than a century as wards of the state, the Nisga'a people – empowered by the self-government provisions of the treaty – are rebuilding our nation. We are taking control of our destiny once again.

———

[S]elf-government means having the freedom to live by our traditions – and to live with the consequences of the decisions we make. It means we are free to prosper by our own hand and ingenuity. It means we are no longer tenants on our own land – we are masters in our own houses once again.

At long last, we are free to make mistakes and to take part in that popular pastime of all free peoples: The right to complain about our elected officials and the right to vote them out of office if we don't like what we see.

———

How do you measure the wealth of a people?

Gross Domestic Product? Productivity? Debt–equity ratio?

Like the Nisga'a Nation, communities around the world are beginning to question the criteria for success imposed by outsiders. We have developed our own ways of measuring the wealth and wellbeing of our people. Unless "success" is defined by those who seek it, it will remain an illusive goal, an objective devised and judged by someone else, far removed.

*March 3, 2003*

# 2005

# TAIAIAKE ALFRED

**Wasáse: Indigenous Pathways of Action and Freedom**

*Taiaiake Alfred is a Kanien'kehaka (Mohawk) and a longtime professor at the University of Victoria. He insists that without a spiritual revolution, political victories will lead nowhere. Wherever he goes across Canada, crowds of young First Nations students gather. What he calls for is not easy. It is in the mind. In the way of life. In the use of language. It is not what politicians or civil servants like to hear, precisely because it is not easy. Perhaps that is the guarantee of its authority.*

There are many differences among the peoples that are indigenous to this land, yet the challenge facing all Onkwehonwe is the same: regaining freedom and becoming self-sufficient by confronting the disconnection and fear at the core of our existence under colonial dominion. We are separated from the sources of our goodness and power: from each other, our cultures, and our lands. These connections must be restored. Governmental power is founded on fear, which is used to control and manipulate us in many ways; so, the strategy must be to confront fear and display the courage to act against and defeat the state's power.

The first question that arises when this idea is applied in a practical way to the situations facing Onkwehonwe in real life is this: How can we regenerate ourselves culturally and achieve freedom and political independence when the legacies of disconnection, dependency, and dispossession have such a strong hold on us? Undeniably, we face a difficult situation. The political and social institutions that govern us have been shaped and organized to serve white power and they conform to the interests of the states founded on that objective. These states and Settler-serving institutions are useless to the cause of our survival, and if we are to free ourselves from the grip of colonialism, we must reconfigure our politics and replace all of the strategies, institutions, and leaders in place today. The transformation will begin inside each one of us as personal change, but decolonization will become a reality only when we collectively both commit to a movement based on an ethical and political vision and consciously reject the colonial postures of weak submission, victimry, and raging violence. It is a political vision and solution that will be capable of altering power relations and rearranging the forces that shape our lives. Politics is the force that channels social, cultural, and economic powers and makes them imminent in our lives. Abstaining from politics is like turning your back on a beast when it is angry and intent on ripping your guts out.

———

Using violence to advance our objectives would lead to frustration and failure for political and military reasons, but it would also falter for deeper spiritual and cultural reasons. I find it very difficult to see any value in asking our future generations to form their identities on and live lives of aggression, would this not validate and maintain the enemy colonizer as an omnipresent and superior reality of our existence for generations to come? This is not the legacy we want to leave for our children. To remain true to a struggle conceived within Onkwehonwe values, the end goal of our Wasáse – our warrior's dance – must be formulated as a spiritual revolution, a culturally rooted *social* movement that transforms the whole of society and a *political* action that seeks to remake the entire landscape of power and relationship to reflect truly a liberated post-imperial vision.

Wasáse is spiritual revolution and contention. It is not a path to violence. And yet, this commitment to non-violence is not pacifism either. This is an important point to make clear: I believe there is a need for morally grounded defiance and non-violent agitation combined with the development of a collective capacity for self-defence, so as to generate within the Settler society a reason and incentive to negotiate constructively in the interest of achieving a respectful coexistence.

# 2006

# JIM DUMONT

## Indigenous Intelligence

*For many years Jim Dumont, an Anishinaabe thinker, was
a senior professor at Laurentian University in Sudbury. Is he
a philosopher or a spiritual leader? Is there a difference? Here,
in fragments from his Inaugural J.W.E. Newbery Lecture,
he opposes the indigenous idea of civilization as a circular
concept to the Western analytic and linear approach.*

The Creator drew a circle on the darkness, and that was the
first work of art. He thereby created the way by which all
of creative activity would unfold – in a circular manner. And
so everything is circular in our worldview. It is understandable within the circle. When life moves out equally in the four
directions, it forms a perfect circle. Each of those energies that
cause the circle to move equally in each direction is a different
energy. So, the energies of the four directions is what holds
all of life together in the great circle of life's unfolding. Thus it
was established for all time that the circle would be the way in
which all life unfolds as it moves forever towards the creation
and re-creation of life.

———

The view that life is circular, after all, is *far* more intelligent than saying: "Everything happens in a linear sequence; that there is a beginning and there is an end. You are born here and you are dead there and that there are these steps that you take in between." In my estimation that is almost an infantile view of reality; and yet, that is supposed to be the most intelligent view. It is puzzling how we have been talked into getting rid of our own circular view to be replaced by something that is far inferior to our original way of thinking.

———

The Circle, then, being primary, influences, in every way, how we see the world. In the process of how life evolves – how the natural world grows and works together, how all things move toward their destiny while changing from one stage to another – the circle should be evidenced everywhere we look.

———

*Harmony* is the manner by which the Creator achieved creation.... *Balance* is a fundamental principle within the way that harmony in interrelationship works.... All of this does not presume that there is balance, equilibrium and symmetry everywhere and at all times in the world. The opposites or twin of each of these exist simultaneously in our reality. The key here is that our reality is *predisposed toward achieving balance* and prefers it.... Human beings, trying to live effectively and qualitatively in this world, will naturally and intelligently espouse the value of *desire for harmony* in all forms of interrelationship.

———

The prevailing and dominating worldview that surrounds us today and to which we are compelled to respond is one that is narrow in its vision, exclusive and detached in relating to the total environment, analytical and deductive in its perception and thinking, linear in its doing, and hierarchical and competitive in its management of the field of activity.

By Indigenous standards of *intelligence*, the accepted limitations to perception, the lack of consideration and caring for the total environment, the restrictions of thinking to narrow confines of cerebral activity, and the confinement to narrowly defined boundaries in the rational, scientific paradigm of the Euro-western tradition, are ways of seeing, relating, thinking, and doing that are deficient in most of the qualities of higher *intelligence*.

*October 18, 2006*

# 2009

# SIILA WATT-CLOUTIER

**Returning Canada to a Path of Principle**
The LaFontaine–Baldwin Lecture

*Here is one of our most powerful advocates for sensible
climate-change policies. Siila Watt-Cloutier is Inuk,
originally from Nunavik, now from Nunavut. She has
been the elected international chair of the Inuit Circumpolar
Council.*

*In 2009 she became the second Aboriginal intellectual
to give the LaFontaine–Baldwin Lecture. Georges Erasmus
was the first. She spoke in Iqaluit. It was the first time one of
Canada's major national lectures had been delivered from the
Arctic — from the Arctic to the south. Five hundred people
jammed into the Inuksuk High School gym. The governor
general was there, the former governor general, all the
lieutenant governors, the premier of Nunavut, her Cabinet.
A section at the front was reserved for elders. There were
students, hunters, the community at large. Her speech was
streamed by Zacharias Kunuk's IsumaTV to various theatres
across Canada.*

Northern Canada faces many challenges. How we respond to them will reveal the sort of democracy we are creating in the northern half of the continent in this still-new millennium. While most Canadians live in the south, close to the border with the United States, Canada remains an Arctic nation and every day the Arctic looms larger in our consciousness. That is understandable as, increasingly, what happens here in the Arctic will colour Canada's approach to the rest of the world.

———

Inuit have a great responsibility. We occupy a unique position in Canadian society and, increasingly, in world affairs. As the Arctic becomes globally important, Inuit too are at a turning point or a crossroads in our development as a people – an Indigenous people – within this great country we call Canada.

———

Inuit are a uniquely adaptable people. We have weathered the storm of modernization remarkably well. Inuit in Canada have gone from dog-teams and igluvigaks, the Inuktitut term for igloo, to snowmobiles, jumbo jets, permanent homes, and even supermarkets, all within the past 50 years. Understandably, the speed in which these enormous changes happened knocked us off balance. We used to be the most independent and self-sufficient of Peoples, but we lost much control over our lives as a result of tumultuous change and multiple historical traumas.

Many families from specific communities were forcibly relocated to new communities not of their choosing in the name of sovereignty. They were the first to assert sovereignty for Canada.

———

Political agitation by non-governmental groups who had never visited and completely misunderstood our communities, aided by compliant politicians, caused the collapse of our sealskin economy with hugely negative social consequences and here we go again with round two of that misguided, emotionally driven campaign which again only brings hardship to our Inuit world.

All of these processes resulted in a serious failure of Canadian democracy to advance the public good. Our governments themselves as they functioned from their own ignorance and colonial arrogance led us, as Inuit, astray from our own principled ways.

In addition, together these traumatic events deeply wounded and dispirited many, translating into "collective pain" experienced by families and communities alike.

———

One way of life does not have to be at the cost of another. In fact many Inuit who are connected to the values, principles, traditions, and wisdom of our traditional culture are better equipped and able to balance more effectively the two worlds. This important insight should be reflected in our public policies and programs toward the Arctic.

———

Slowing down climate change would be the best long-term solution to enforcing Canada's Arctic sovereignty. Instead of aggressively dealing with climate change and becoming an international leader in these global efforts, Canada has decided that the best way to defend its Arctic sovereignty is with the military through a new fleet of armed ice breakers. Canada, a peaceful nation, will now "defend" the Arctic.

Canada should take another approach – a more principled and human-centred approach. As a great Canadian, Lloyd Axworthy, has advocated, and as I have suggested before, Canada should take the lead in the peaceful, cooperative management of the Arctic. Canada should take a relentlessly co-operative approach. To focus international attention and debate we should consider promoting new multilateral institutions, or greatly expanding the role of the eight-nation Arctic Council, which was established in 1996 largely as a Canadian foreign policy initiative.

———

As wise stewards of our land, I would urge my own people to refuse the dangerous compromises between our principles and development that might diminish our own moral standing and claim to high ground as indigenous peoples. As we call on the world to change its ecologically degrading practices, we must not accept those practices at home no matter how desperate our need for jobs or economic development. Economic gain must not override the existence and well being of a whole people whose way of life is already being severely taxed. We must not let the prospect of development in the Arctic diminish our ability and our region's ability to teach the "life-centred sustainability" that Arctic Peoples have practised for millennia. The people whose lives depend upon the ice and snow for cultural survival must be a central component of all our plans. We must not permit the discussion of northern development to be conducted only in terms of sovereignty, resources, and economics. The focus must be on the human dimension, human communities and protection of human cultural rights.

———

Every level of the governance system here in the North must be mobilized to ensure that Indigenous knowledge and wisdom is the foundation of sustainable economic endeavour.

Nakuqmiik

*May 29, 2009*
*The 9th LaFontaine–Baldwin Lecture*
*The Institute for Canadian Citizenship*

# 2011

# E. RICHARD ATLEO (UMEEK)

## Principles of Tsawalk: An Indigenous Approach to Global Crisis

E. Richard Atleo (Umeek) is hereditary chief of the Ahousaht
First Nation on the west coast of Vancouver Island. He
is also a professor at the University of Manitoba, the first
Aboriginal awarded a PhD in British Columbia, and above
all, a very interesting philosopher. In his two books on
Tsawalk he lays out an Ahousaht world view.

Tsawalk is an overarching theory of harmony — All is
one. In Western terms we might call it a humanist theory.
And as Atleo says, there are concepts shared with Western
humanism. But this is not a Western theory. It is philosophy
as a way of life, understood to be shared by a people.

Here he writes about the practical reality of myths and
the relationship between gifts and social harmony. It was
this gift giving, through the potlatch, that the Canadian
government banned in 1884 as inappropriate in the world
of the Protestant work ethic. What they were banning was
another world view.

## On the Role of Myth

Although myths appear to focus upon the non-physical or spiritual, they comprise stories that are meant to be practical. They are meant as guides to understanding the nature of reality. In this sense, myths are not necessarily in opposition to the intent of scientific inquiry; rather, they simply take a different route and employ different terminology. Whereas scientific inquiry depends on theory, indigenous knowledge systems depend on myths. Both theory and myths can be tested. The Nuu-chah-nulth test is called the ʔuusumč, the vision quest. It can truly be said that, for the Nuu-chah-nulth, as a research process the ʔuusumč is rooted in, and validated by, lived experience. Consequently, when ʔuusumč was practised universally, as it was in precontact Nuu-chah-nulth society, it could unveil truths about the nature of reality that were so reliable that they sustained a way of life over millennia. If the foundation for a perspective on reality is untrue, then there is no possibility that it can have a practical application. What people believe and practise must have enough practical substance that it enables them to survive, to live adequately, and even to thrive.

———

In *Tsawalk* I suggest that myths – or origin stories, as I prefer to call them – serve the same purpose as does scientific theory since they provide insight into the nature of existence.

From a Nuu-chah-nulth perspective, myths are a reflection of, and a source of wisdom about, the nature of reality. They are also of mysterious origin. Yet, it can be deduced from the meaning of the name of Kwaaʔuuc, Owner of All, that they may well be the ultimate source of Nuu-chah-nulth knowledge. Myths originate with Kwaaʔuuc. This is something believed but it is also something that can be neither proved nor disproved with existing research tools. This belief is no less sound than are current scientific "beliefs" about string theory, parallel universes, and other theories about the nature of reality that cannot be proved or disproved with existing research tools.

———

A constellation of teachings was developed to maintain and to enhance life's major purpose, namely, the development of harmonious relationships between and among all life forms. These teachings applied to every category and dimension of life, whether within an extended family, between nations, or between all other life forms, including those life forms (such as plants and animals) that are now considered to be simply resources. These teachings also applied to the relationship between the physical and the spiritual realms.

———

### On Gift Giving and Harmony

Why is it that gift giving is the core of the Nuu-chah-nulth feasts to which visitors from other communities have been invited? And why does the speaker for the host of such feasts, when he calls out the name of one of these visitors, present a gift with words that can be translated into English as: "You have been recognized"? At ceremonial feasts, why is it important to recognize those who have been invited? One answer is that the act of recognition has been found to be an effective way of negotiating a reality that seems to range from the utter destructiveness at one end to sublime harmony at the other.

———

Over time it was learned that gift giving and recognition promoted balance and harmony between beings, that it obeyed what might be called the laws of the positive side of polarity. To neglect the promotion of balance and harmony between beings promoted what might be referred to as the laws of the negative side of polarity. These are not new ideas. Indeed, they are commonly held both by Western and Eastern morality (generosity begets generosity) and by the laws of physics (to every action there is a reaction). When two neighbouring nations shared the same resources, whether cedar, salmon, or human, then it was obvious to the ancient Nuu-chah-nulth that to neglect the act of recognition would open the way to conflict, while to observe the act of recognition, through what I refer to as "mutual concern," would open the way to balance and harmony.

## 2012

# WAB KINEW

### Idle No More Is Not Just an "Indian Thing"

*Idle No More was a moment — a large moment — that seemed
to catch most people by surprise. Why? Because the moment
was real. We have become used to scripted political events,
false public emotions, the lowest forms of rhetoric. Here was a
moment unfolding over several months that was not planned,
not top down. Wab Kinew, a member of the Midewin, lives
in Winnipeg. He is one of the most impressive figures in the
Aboriginal comeback.*

*During the winter events of 2012–2013, the media, the
politicians, the technocracy kept asking, "What does all this
mean?" On December 17, 2012, in* The Huffington Post,
*Kinew gave an answer so solid that any of the confused media,
politicians and technocrats could understand, if they wished.*

*It is a matter of learning how to listen to the indigenous
narrative, which in good part could also be ours. Kinew
wrote as he speaks, in a voice clear and strong, anchored in
history and solid as to what can and needs to be done.*

*His essay was reprinted in* The Winter We Danced,
*a remarkable anthology that captures the many voices of
2012–2013.*

What is "Idle No More"?

It is a loosely knit political movement encompassing rallies drawing thousands of people across dozens of cities, road blocks, a shoving match on Parliament Hill between chiefs and mounties and one high profile hunger strike.

It is also a meme tweeted and shared about thousands of times a day, for messages about indigenous rights, indigenous culture and cheap indigenous jokes ("Turn off your ignition #idlenomore").

The name Idle No More comes from a recent meeting in Saskatchewan. Sylvia McAdam and three others were mad about Bill C-45, the omnibus budget bill. Their biggest frustration was that nobody seemed to be talking about it. Two provisions in particular upset them: the reduction in the amount of federally protected waterways and a fast-tracked process to surrender reserve lands. In McAdam's view, if Aboriginal people did not speak out it would mean they "comply with [their] silence." So she and her friends decided to speak out. They would be "Idle No More." They held an information session under the same name. Co-organizer Tanya Kappo fired off a tweet with the hashtag "#IdleNoMore."

#IdleNoMore struck a nerve. Though Bill C-45 has become law, many Aboriginal people have voiced their opposition to it. Many of the other tensions in the indigenous community have started to bubble up to the surface, and "Idle No More" now encompasses a broad conversation calling for recognition of treaty rights, revitalization of indigenous cultures and an end to legislation imposed without meaningful consultation.

To me this conversation is more than just an "Indian Thing." It is one that Canadians of all backgrounds should pay attention to, if not participate in. The ideals that are underlying this action are ones to which we all aspire, even if we may disagree on how exactly to pursue them.

## 5. #IdleNoMore Is about Engaging Youth

When Grand Chief Derek Nepinak went on national television after he and some other leaders got into that shoving match outside the chamber, he acknowledged the Chiefs were responding to young people calling for action via social media. At the rallies held in cities like Winnipeg, Windsor and Edmonton, it has been the youth who have done the organizing, and it has been the youth who have made up the majority of attendees. Scanning Facebook and Twitter, "#IdleNoMore" has popped up in the timelines of people who typically discuss Snooki or the Kardashians. Agree or disagree with the message, Idle No More has accomplished something all Canadians want: it has young people paying attention to politics.

## 4. #IdleNoMore Is about Finding Meaning

Much of the talk around Idle No More is about preserving indigenous culture, either by revitalizing spiritual practices or by keeping intact what little land base we have left. The reason culture is so important is that it provides a way to grapple with the big questions in life: "Who am I?," "What am I doing here?" and "What happens after I die?" Some of the answers have been handed down as words of wisdom. Other times, you are told to go out on to the land and discover them for yourself through fasting or prayer. We need these ways. As I look around and see many fellow Canadians searching for meaning in their own lives, I think to myself perhaps they could use these ways as well.

### 3. #IdleNoMore Is about Rights
What almost everyone carrying the Idle No More banner is calling for is meaningful consultation between the federal government and First Nations people. This is what section 35 of our constitution is all about: Aboriginal and treaty rights are recognized and affirmed, and that means we have to talk. If there is no meaningful conversation happening, it is troublesome. Aboriginal people may be the canary in the coal mine. If we overlook one section of the constitution does that mean others are in similar jeopardy?

### 2. #IdleNoMore Is about the Environment
Idle No More started in part because of outrage that Bill C-45 reduced the number of federally protected waterways. The environment continues to be a regular topic at Idle No More protests. Dr. Pam Palmater, one of the leading voices in the Idle No More conversation, argues this indigenous environmentalism is significant since the Crown has a duty to consult with Aboriginal people before natural resource projects proceed. She says, "First Nations are Canadians' last, best

hope of protecting the land, water, sky and plants and animals for their future generations as well."

## 1. #IdleNoMore Is about Democracy

Democracy thrives when well-informed people are engaged and make their voices heard. Idle No More started with four young lawyers trying to inform the people in their communities about an issue they were passionate about. Now many people are engaged. Even more information is being shared, and even more voices are being heard. There is no one leader or "list of demands" attributable to Idle No More. While this may seem chaotic, this is what democracy is all about. Democracy is messy. Democracy is loud. Democracy is about hearing a wide range of voices and trying to build a path forward among them. It is not about shutting off debate or trying to rush things in through the back door.

# 2013

# JEAN TEILLET

## On the Manitoba Métis Victory

*Within the great story of the Aboriginal comeback there are
emblematic struggles that tell us how it is all going. One of
the most important has been the long battle of the Manitoba
Métis, from the 1860s on, to keep their land, to get their land
back, to have Canada accept that it is their land. In 2013 the
Supreme Court ruled in favour of the Métis. It was a great
victory for justice in the broadest sense, because the whole
question was tied to the government's intentional misuse of its
power. Whether the Government of Canada will now honour
its obligations is the next question.*

*Jean Teillet, Louis Riel's great-grandniece, has played
a central role in many historic indigenous cases. I think
Riel, who to the despair of his lawyers defended himself so
movingly in his own trial, would be particularly proud that
one of his descendants has been important in so many of the
court decisions that are giving Canada a new equilibrium.*

In 1868 the new Canadian government was negotiating
with Great Britain for the transfer of Rupert's Land and the
Northwest Territories. While Great Britain raised the issue of

the resident aboriginal peoples and insisted that its policies and responsibilities be transferred along with the land, it occurred to neither party to include the Indians or Métis in their negotiations.

It is this land and resource transfer that sparked the events of 1869–70 in Red River that were made famous by Louis Riel. To resolve the dispute, Riel's negotiators agreed that existing Métis land holdings (the long river lots) would be affirmed and that 1,400,000 acres of land would be set aside for the Métis children. Why for the children? Because Riel knew that in a few short years thousands of English-speaking farmers would come into the Red River Valley from Ontario. Riel wanted a head start for Métis youth and he believed that land would provide that head start. The agreement to provide land to the children was put into s. 31 of the Manitoba Act, 1870. That Act later became part of the Canadian Constitution, which had the effect of giving constitutional protection to the promises made to the Métis. It was on the basis of that promise that the Métis laid down their arms and agreed to enter into the compact of Confederation.

Unfortunately, the promise was broken. Canada delayed for 15 years. In that time, the anticipated thousands of immigrants arrived and scooped up the best land. The Métis children did not actually receive the lands. They certainly received no head start. Indeed such was the post-1870 anti-Métis reign of terror in Red River – rapes, tarring and feathering, assaults, murder – that many Métis fled to Saskatchewan. Their arrival set the stage for the events of 1885 and the Riel Resistance. But that's another story for another time.

The Manitoba Métis Federation case was about the broken Manitoba Act promises. The case was launched in 1981, delayed in hopes of resolution by the patriation of the Constitution in 1982, Meech Lake in 1987 and Charlottetown in 1992, but eventually reinvigorated, and now finally, we have a decision by the Supreme Court of Canada.

What did the court say? They said that Canada had breached its honour of the Crown duty in failing to provide the lands to the Métis children in a timely way that would be consistent with its constitutional promise. The court said that Canada had unfinished business with the Métis. This is clearly a victory.

As an aside, I note that this is a case that touches me closely because, as you all know, I am the great grand niece of Louis Riel and the lands at issue include my family's lands.

But what does the case mean in practical terms? What do we do with this result? My own thought is that we have been handed a new shiny tool. Unfortunately, we don't yet know what it can do. We think we might build something with it, but what should we build? What materials do we use? Who will build it? Where will we build it? There will be a lot of time required to prepare for this new tool. And this is not necessarily bad or unusual. After First Nations won the Calder case in 1973 (that's the case where the court first held that aboriginal title existed), it was 1978 before Canada announced its then new modern treaty process in response. So it will take years for this to get properly started and many more for results. The take-home point is this – government moves slowly at the best of times and at a glacial pace when it is moving reluctantly. So the Métis task is to keep their feet to the fire. This will require consistent pressure from our politicians and possibly another court case. But don't lose hope.

Government is in a bit of a bind. The court found them in breach of their constitutional obligations. So they know they have to do something to remedy that. They also know that the principal reason for the breach was the 15-year delay. So they know they cannot delay for that long. Likely at this point they have no idea what they should do and because they are by nature secretive, it is likely that we won't know what they have decided until after the fact. But take heart! The shiny new tool has some power to effect change. Our task is to decide what we want and then to assert the necessary pressure to make it so.

My suggestion? We should start with an "ask" of 1,400,000 acres of land. This is not an outrageous "ask" because this is what we were deprived of and also because Canada is rich in land. This "ask" should form the basis for our negotiated settlement. If indeed, as the Supreme Court of Canada has noted, we are all here to stay, then the Métis (who despite being partners in Confederation are the only landless aboriginal people) should have a land base restored to them. If we did not get the "head start" lands in the 19th century, we could press the re-start button with lands provided in the 21st century.

Métis are clearly on the rise again. Everywhere I go I can see it. We are becoming better educated, we are taking political reins in our hands again, we are taking charge of our own lives and again becoming a force to reckon with. The Manitoba Métis Federation case adds a significant tool into our toolbox. Let's see what we can make of this new start for our children and our children's children.

# KATHRYN TENEESE
# CHAIR, KTUNAXA NATION COUNCIL

## On Reconciliation and Modernity

*I heard Chair Kathryn Teneese say these words at a
gathering in the Columbia River Basin. The Columbia
River Treaty runs until 2024. As of 2014 the process of
renegotiations can begin. Chair Teneese of the Ktunaxa
Nation Council is a widely respected leader. Her approach is
careful and clear.*

*She is also one of the leaders in the battle to prevent the
development of the "Jumbo Glacier Resort" in the Qat'muk
area. Among many things, this is a Grizzly Bear reserve.
But Chair Teneese and the Ktunaxa see it in the broader
context as the home of the Grizzly Bear Spirit: "Qat'muk
is of profound spiritual and cultural importance to our
nation." Some people will find this soft or vague, but they are
missing the underlying argument that environmentalism is
not about humans deciding what will live or die. It is about
understanding a relationship in which humans are part of the
environment.*

There are certain things that are different about the human beings that we are. For example, there is the fact that we have a connection to our homelands, not in the same way that others do who have chosen to live in our homelands. That's not a bad thing. All it needs is to be acknowledged and recognized. So often I think that any movement forward has to come from a place of acknowledgment and recognition. Instead there is a notion of denial that continues to exist today. We still have Supreme Court of Canada cases in which the premise of the government's factums, which they table before the court action, are based on a denial of our existence. How many times do the Nuu-chah-nulth have to prove who they are before they can even talk about their right to sell fish? How many times do the Tsilhqot'in have to prove who they are before they can talk about their connection to their homeland?

That is the kind of narrative which has been accepted. That it's ok for the people in places of power to start a conversation by denying.

Each and every one of us can do something about that. We can make the case and say to the people sitting in those positions of power: "That is unacceptable. You cannot continue to do that on my behalf."

Essentially that is what they're doing. If you don't say anything, you're condoning it and making it ok. The point I am making is that activities and events, reconciliation do not make. Reconciliation is not an event, you know. It's something that needs to enter into the way we do things. Think of this past week in Vancouver, where we had the week of reconciliation which culminated in the walk that 70,000 people participated in, despite a downpour of rain. And while that isn't going to fix everything, it certainly meant that those non-Aboriginal people who took part in that event had begun to change their narrative. It was a small thing, but they started. I think one needs to find ways, small ways, the baby steps, because we didn't get to the relationship we have here overnight. We need to find the way that we can do things together that makes sense. And that's really what it comes down to. It's about making sense. It's about common sense. We all talk about that, but a lot of times things that we do really aren't very sensible.

―――――――

This is a time when we need to think about how something would have worked a hundred years ago, two hundred years ago, three hundred years ago. But we also need to recognize that we're not stuck in time. That's another fallacy I find when I'm asked to make comments. Very often it's ok for me to talk from a historical perspective. *But don't you dare talk about how you fit into contemporary issues. We don't want that. We don't want to hear that. We like you in your beads, we like you in your buckskins. We like you that way. We like you when you do the "Hula"* – that's what I call it – *but don't talk about us in a way that makes us uncomfortable. Don't remind us of things that make us uncomfortable.* But, you know, it's ok if we drum. It's acceptable.

When we start talking the other way, it causes discomfort for some people. Not everyone. The other thing is that the whole "romantic notion" is sometimes also a challenge – the "romantic notion" that everything is perfect. Nothing is perfect. I mean it depends on one's definition of "perfection."

So, we have to recognize that as a society – because that's what we are – we need to be caring about where it is that we want to go.

# 2013

# NIIGAANWEWIDAM JAMES SINCLAIR

## The Words We Have Inherited

On January 14, 2013, the Morris Mirror, a small
newspaper in the small Manitoba town of Morris, published
a racist editorial in reaction to the Idle No More movement.
These natives, the editor-in-chief, Reed Turcotte, wrote,
"are demanding unrealistic expectations of the government
and . . . in some cases, natives are acting like terrorists in their
own country. Indians/natives want it all but corruption and
laziness prevent some of them from working for it."

Sometimes stupidity of this sort offers all of us an
opportunity. Niigaan Sinclair, Anishinaabe, professor at
the University of Manitoba, editor of Manitowapow, and
part of the Kino-nda-niimi Collective that produced The
Winter We Danced anthology, is an important voice in the
Aboriginal comeback.

He wrote a remarkable letter to the Morris Mirror editor.
You could say that he dropped a boulder on a grain of sand.
But Sinclair understood the implications of such an editorial
being left unanswered. And so on January 22 he drove to
Morris to talk with Turcotte. The offices of the newspaper were

*locked and Turcotte refused to see him. Eventually Sinclair attached his letter to the door of the newspaper's office.*

*Read it. In these few words everything is said. What came to my mind was Luther nailing his Ninety-Five Theses to the door of All Saints' Church in Wittenberg, a German city in Saxony. A provincial church. A provincial town. The beginning of the Reformation.*

*In truth, the Reformation was already underway, as was the Aboriginal revival, as was Idle No More. But there is something absolutely right about the drama of nailing philosophy to a public door. And the quality of the letter speaks for itself.*

To the Editor of the Morris Mirror,

I want to give you something.

A gift. A story, maybe.

A piece of our home.

I offer this in the way I would bring food to a feast – if you and your family organized that sort of thing – and invited my family and I to enjoy all we had brought.

This is, perhaps, an unlikely vision – but I offer it nonetheless.

I give this so that you might know a little about the land where you and I now reside. The earth, water, and wind have seen far more than you or I – and will be here far after we have gone. They have witnessed far better than us.

I also give this as a rejection of what has passed for communication in our home: a cacophony of anonymous, Internet commentaries with name-calling and tired, predictable stereotypes based on little more than a passing glance. In editorials, rich in generalizations and lacking in accuracy.

I give this so that we might find a way to live together

meaningfully, in the vision established by the agreement that made this place. This is a treaty that – while never fulfilled – promises mutual benefit, non-interference, and peace. These are words promised by the man who your town is named after, Alexander Morris. As Morris and those who oversaw the formation and delivery of Treaty One remind us: the vision of this agreement is a map marked with signposts of honesty, bravery, patience, and listening. We now have to trust that these are still there – even if the brush has grown over them.

I give this to ask you to consider what could make a human being come to be seen as "lazy" and "corrupt."

I ask you whether these traits are some inherent, savage deficiency or the product of a constant barrage of words driven by the belief that second-rate, dying cultures exist. That these words became laws that locked people into unsustainable areas, made it impossible to make a living, and threw them in jail if they resisted. I ask you to think about those who promised much during treaty time and then supplied their friends with handfuls of welfare, told them how to run their community and then, finally, removed their children and put them into schools where they were physically and emotionally abused. These children learned that they were inferior and how important it was to destroy the languages and cultures they came from. Many resisted, but were left with the gap of years away from their parents and communities. Returning home, if any did, there were understandable feelings of confusion and disjunction.

I ask you to think about how, at the same time and in schools nearby, Canadian children learned the same curriculum and that they were superior. These children were taught the same words as what the other children endured: they were abused too.

I ask how you or your children might have turned out if any of this happened to you. Now, call them "lazy" and "corrupt."

Human beings are obviously more than this.

I give this to you to honour a grandfather who fought for this country, lying about his age so he didn't have to return to residential school, and was injured, never to be healed again. I give this to recall how the government he fought for abandoned him and told him he was no longer an Indian. How he was left completely on his own, to struggle with alcohol and disability, with children to feed and bills to pay. I have no doubt that for Grandpa the vision of the treaty that promised him much was a blurry sight. It was probably made invisible when he lost the only woman he ever truly loved to illness and his first son was killed by Canadians who were never punished.

I give this to you to ask whether dependency is more about those dependent, or those who created the system of dependence. I ask where most questions need to be asked: to those who benefit incredibly through privilege and exploitation, or to those who trust promises and endure more about repairing the imbalance. Whether it is to those who hand systems of dominance to their children, or those invested in escaping this abusive relationship. Whether it is to those who want to call people dancing in a mall "terrorists," or to those who want to find another way, another path.

I give this to you to remember a man who quit drinking when his grandson was born. This man, defined by so many as broken, lazy, and dangerous, chose to give this little boy the greatest gift he could give: love. He gave it not in the hopes that he could repair the past but that he could give him a chance to see something better, something beautiful. Something more than the violence that had been rained down on him. This man, a member of Treaty One – just like you and I – chose to end cycles that had shaped so much of his life. This man chose to stand up, to be more than words and policies, and to tell a new story. I know this. I'm living it.

It is time that we all learn a little history about who we are and maybe, if we're lucky, make some new paths. I believe that we are more than the words and images we have inherited. I know that we can make a better home than this, that we can expect more of ourselves if we are brave, honest, patient, and if we listen. It is time that we give each other gifts of responsibility.

I ask you to be more than the words we have inherited.

And, I ask you to talk. Share food. Discuss how we can be more.

You have said that you are not ready. That's OK. Change is hard. I am ready.

I will wait for you.

Our home is too important.

Miigwech, ekosi, thanks, merci.

Niisha Wkc wrapped in a blanket made by her mother to symbolize the four directions. It is a blanket of ceremony and prayer. © Zack Embree.

# NOTES

## I. HISTORY IS UPON US

**p. 8 Francis Pegahmagabow (1891–1952), third generation**
Adrian Hayes, *Pegahmagabow, Life-Long Warrior* (Toronto: Blue Butterfly Books, 2009).
Joseph Boyden, *Three Day Road* (Toronto: Penguin Group Canada, 2006).

**p. 9 E. Richard Atleo (Umeek) eloquently describes**
E. Richard Atleo (Umeek), *Principles of Tsawalk* (Vancouver: UBC Press, 2011), 96.

**p. 12 Myriad laws, regulations and administrative structures**
Canada. Law and Government Division. *Aboriginal People: History of Discriminatory Laws*, Wendy Moss and Elaine Gardner O'Toole, eds., November 1987; revised November 1991; updated 2002, 2–16.

**p. 13 Dances outside of any individual's own reserve**
Canada. Parliament of Canada. *The Indian Act*, R.S.C., 1927, 98, s. 140, paras 1–3 and s. 141.

**p. 13 We broke our own laws**
Canada. Parliament of Canada. *The Indian Act*, R.S.C., 1927, 98, s. 140. Until real changes are made in national policy we should call this department by its old name: Indian Affairs.

This department has had nine names since Confederation, usually mixed in with commodities, as in National Resources. The use of the words *Indian Affairs* refers to the R.S.C., 1985, c. I-5 legislation – the Indian Act. This is still the case even if a new administrative or *applied* name has been used since 2011: Aboriginal Affairs and Northern Development Canada. Legally speaking, it is still the Department of Indian Affairs.

Departments that have been responsible for Indian Affairs:

- The Departments of the Secretary of State of Canada (to 1869)
- The Department of the Secretary of State for the Provinces (1869–1873)
- The Department of the Interior (1873–1880)
- The Department of Indian Affairs (1880–1936)
- The Department of Mines and Resources (1936–1950)
- The Department of Citizenship and Immigration (1950–1965)
- The Department of Northern Affairs and National Resources (1966)
- The Department of Indian Affairs and Northern Development (1966 to present) (Applied title as of 2011: Aboriginal Affairs and Northern Development Canada)

The departments that have been responsible for Northern Affairs:

- The Department of the Interior (1873–1936)
- The Department of Mines and Resources (1936–1950)
- The Department of Resources and Development (1950–1953)
- The Department of Northern Affairs and National Resources (1953–1966)
- The Department of Indian Affairs and Northern Development (1966 to present) (Applied title as of 2011: Aboriginal Affairs and Northern Development Canada)

**p. 14 One of the most eloquent summaries of the situation**
Memorial to Sir Wilfrid Laurier, Premier of the Dominion
of Canada, from the Chiefs of the Shuswap, Okanagan and
Couteau Tribes of British Columbia, delivered to him in
Kamloops, B.C., on August 25, 1910.

## III. WORKING TO AVOID JUSTICE

**p. 25 But the most important handout was to us**
James Daschuk, *Clearing the Plains: Disease, Politics of Starvation, and
the Loss of Aboriginal Life* (Regina: University of Regina Press, 2013).

**p. 25 Bob Rae put it this way**
The Honourable Bob Rae (closing keynote address, "As Long
as the Rivers Flow: Coming Back to the Treaty Relationship in
Our Time" conference, June 1, 2014, Fort McMurray, Alberta).

## IV. AUTHORITY VERSUS POWER

**p. 35 Thomas King presents an accurate**
Thomas King, *The Inconvenient Indian: A Curious Account of Native
People in North America* (Toronto: Random House of Canada,
2012).

**p. 38 "… the reconciliation of the pre-existence of Aboriginal
societies**
Canada. British Columbia. Supreme Court Judgments.
*Delgamuukw v. British Columbia (1997)*, 3 *S.C.R.* 1010. British
Columbia, 1997, http://scc-csc.lexum.com/scc-csc/scc-csc/en/
item/1569/index.do.

**p. 39 None has succeeded**
To understand the story fully, read a sample of the following
key documents:
Charlie Angus, MP, "Failure to Seek and Disclose Evidence in
St. Anne's Residential Abuse Scandal" (letters to Peter MacKay,
Federal Attorney General, July 21 and November 25, 2013).
Seetal Sunga, "Amendments to St. Anne's IRS Narrative

– Response to Charlie Angus" (email message to Ana Stuhec, Caroline Clark, Janet Brooks, Linda Denis, cc to Catherine Coughlan, Michael Bader, November 26, 2013).

Canada. Ontario. Ontario Superior Court of Justice. Decision of Justice Paul Perell of the Ontario Superior Court of Justice, *Fontaine v. Canada* (Attorney General), 2014 ONSC 283, Court File no. 00-CV–129059, January 14, 2014.

Peter MacKay, Minister of Justice and Attorney General of Canada (letter to Charlie Angus, MP, January 14, 2014).

Edmund Metatawabin, PKKA Coordinator (letter to Hon. Peter MacKay, Minister of Justice and Attorney General of Canada, Fort Albany, Ontario, February 10, 2014).

A useful analysis: Dave Dean, "Our Government Is Withholding Documents Concerning the Torture of Native Children," VICE Canada, July 17, 2013, www.vice.com/en_ca/print/the-canadian-government-is-withholding-documents-concerning-the-torture-of-native-children.

**p. 41 There is no suggestion from the minister of error**
The largest story is laid out by Edmund Metatawabin in *Up Ghost River: A Chief's Journey Through the Turbulent Waters of Native History* (Toronto: Alfred A. Knopf Canada, 2014).

## VII. FORMS OF ARGUMENT

**p. 51 "a bloated, inefficient and unaccountable bureaucracy"**
Ghislain Picard, "It's Ottawa's Turn to Be Transparent," *The Globe and Mail*, August 22, 2014.

**p. 53 Hayden King published a fine analysis**
"First Nations Transparency Act May Do More Harm Than Good: Hayden King," CBC News, August 2, 2014.

## IX. COMING BACK

**p. 66 Edmond Gagne (1921– )**
Métis Nation of Alberta, *Voices of Courage, Alberta Métis Veterans Remembered* (Métis Nation of Alberta, 2006), 29–33.

## XIV. MOVING TO THE STREETS

**p. 103 The first key issue for Aboriginals in C-38**
Canada. Parliament of Canada. First Session, Forty-first
Parliament, 60–61 Elizabeth II, 2011–2012, Statutes of Canada
2012, Ch. 19 [Ottawa, Ont], 2012, www.parl.gc.ca/
housepublications/publication.aspx?DociD=5697420&FILE=4.

**p. 103 The second issue with C-38**
Canada. British Columbia. *The Fisheries Act Canada*, Fisheries Act
R.S.C., 1985, c. F-14. Fish Habitat Protection and Pollution
Prevention [Burnaby, B.C.], 1985.

**p. 104 In C-45 the issue is a weakening of the rules**
Canada. Parliament of Canada. First Session, Forty-first
Parliament, 60–61 Elizabeth II, 2011–2012, Statutes of Canada
2012, Ch. 31 [Ottawa, Ont], 2012, www.parl.gc.ca/content/
hoc/Bills/411/Government/C-45/C-45_4/C-45_4.PDF.

## XV. AN OMNIBUS IS A BUS

**p. 114 In the same year, Bill C-45 was 457 pages**
Janyce McGregor, "22 Changes in the Budget Bill Fine Print:
457-page Omnibus Budget Implementation Bill Amends 64
Different Acts or Regulations," CBC News, October 26, 2012,
www.cbc.ca/m/touch/canada/story/1.1233481.

**p. 114 In twelve months, Parliament was bullied**
Canada. Parliament of Canada. First Session, Forty-
first Parliament, 60–61 Elizabeth II, 2011–2012, House
of Commons Canada 2012, Bill C-45 [Ottawa, Ont],
2012, www.parl.gc.ca/HousePublications/Publication.
aspx?DocId=5765988&Col=1&File=4.

## XVI. BOYS WHO CAN'T COMMIT

**p. 123 focused on technology**
Canada. Prime Minister of Canada's office. "PM announces
launch of the National Research Council Arctic Program."
News [on-line], August 21, 2014.

## XVIII. THE GREAT ISSUE OF OUR TIME

p. 137 "Canada, I believe, is a project of reconciliation
University of Toronto, Faculty of Law, "Chief Justice Beverly
McLachlin Is Guest of Honour for PBSC Law Students," 2014,
www.law.utoronto.ca/news/chief-justice-canada-beverly-
mclachlin-guest-honour-pbscs-law-student-event.

p. 138 "[T]reaty dialogue did not focus on barter
David Arnot, "The Honour of First Nations – The Honour of
the Crown: The Unique Relationship of First Nations with the
Crown" (paper, "The Crown in Canada: Present Realities and
Future Options" conference, Ottawa, June 2010), www.queensu.
ca/iigr/conf/ConferenceOnTheCrown.html.

## XIX. EASY THINGS TO DO

p. 144 One of the most exciting breakthroughs in architecture
Lateral Office, "Arctic Adaptations" Exhibition, 14th
International Architecture Exhibition – La Biennale di Venezia,
2014.

p. 144 At the same time, in *The Walrus*
John van Nostrand, "If We Build It, They Will Stay," *The Walrus*,
September 2013, 34.

## XX. CHOICE

p. 160 "[M]yths are a reflection of
Atleo, 2011, 116.

p. 161 "[I]n the native political and legal system
Jean Friesen, "Magnificent Gifts: The Treaties of Canada with
the Indians of the Northwest 1869–1876," *Transactions of the
Royal Society of Canada*, Series V, Volume 1, 1986, 43–44.

p. 162 James Anaya, reporting on the indigenous situation
James Anaya, "Report of the Special Rapporteur on the Rights
of Indigenous Peoples: The Situation of Indigenous Peoples in
Canada," May 2014. Human Rights Council, UN, 18, 21, 22.

p. 164 "Canada is a test case for a grand notion
A Word from Commissioners, People to People, Nation to Nation:
Highlights from the Report of the Royal Commission on Aboriginal Peoples,
1996, by Co-Chairs René Dussault, j.c.a., Georges Erasmus,
and Commissioners Paul L.A.H. Chartrand, J. Peter Meekison,
Viola Robinson, Mary Sillett, Bertha Wilson (Ottawa:
Aboriginal and Northern Development Canada, 1996), 4.

p. 165 Ovide Mercredi, another remarkable former national
chief: "These two
Ovide Mercredi, in Great Questions of Canada (rev. ed.), Rudyard
Griffiths, ed. (Toronto: Key Porter Books, 2007), 123.

p. 165 E. Richard Atleo (Umeek), who writes about
Atleo, 2011, 80.

p. 166 But we also know that these words were "accepted
Friesen, 1986, 51.

p. 167 Jim Dumont, Indigenous Intelligence
Jim Dumont, "Indigenous Intelligence" (lecture, University of
Sudbury, October 18, 2006). "Indigenous Intelligence," directed
by Daniel Moncion (October 18, 2006), [video recording,
DVD].

p. 168 Leroy Little Bear: "Any individual within a culture
Leroy Little Bear, "Jagged Worldviews Colliding," in Marie
Battiste, Reclaiming Indigenous Voice and Vision (Vancouver: UBC
Press, 2000), 77, 84, 85.

p. 169 Jim Dumont: "The circle, then, being primary
Jim Dumont, 2006.

p. 171 Leroy Little Bear: "The function of Aboriginal
Little Bear, 2000, 81.

p. 172 Leroy Little Bear: "All things are animate
Little Bear, 2000, 77.

p. 172 E. Richard Atleo (Umeek) explains that Western ideas of
democracy
Atleo, 2011, 127.

p. 177 Taiaiake Alfred: "Politics is the force
Taiaiake Alfred, *Indigenous Pathways of Action and Freedom*
(Peterborough: Broadview Press, 2005), 142.

## OTHER PEOPLE'S WORDS

### 1763 The Royal Proclamation
The Canadian Encyclopedia, "Royal Proclamation of 1763 for the
Administration of British Territories in North America" (Ottawa:
The Canadian Encyclopedia), www.thecanadianencyclopedia.ca/
en/article/royal-proclamation-of-1763-/ [June, 2014].

### 1783 Thayendanegea (Joseph Brant) to Sir Frederick Haldimand: A Letter
Charles M. Johnston, ed., *The Valley of the Six Nations: A Collection
of Documents on the Indian Lands of the Grand River* (Toronto:
Champlain Society for the Govt. of Ontario [by] University of
Toronto, 1964), 38–39.

### 1869 Louis Riel, Declaration of the People of Rupert's Land and the North West
Louis Riel, 1-023, "Declaration of the People of Rupert's Land
and the North West. Fort Garry. 69/12/08," in Raymond Huel,
George F.G. Stanley, and D. Litt, eds., *The Collected Writings of
Louis Riel / Les écrits complets de Louis Riel*, Volume 1, 29 December
1861–7 December 1875 (Edmonton: University of Alberta
Press, 1985), 43–44.

### 1884 On the Banning of the Potlatch: House of Commons Debate
House of Commons Debates, "Indian Act Amendment," 5th
Parliament, 2nd Session: Vol. 2, 1884.

## 1910 The Memorial to Sir Wilfrid Laurier, Premier of the Dominion of Canada

Chiefs of the Shuswap, Okanagan and Couteau Tribes of British Columbia, "The Memorial to Sir Wilfrid Laurier, Premier of the Dominion of Canada," 1910, http://shuswapnation.org/to-sir-wilfrid-laurier [June 2014].

## 1927 Amendments to the Indian Act, 1927

Amendments to the Indian Act, R.S., 1927, 98, s. 140, http://mapleleafweb.com/features/the-indian-act-historical-overview.

## 1971 Grand Chief David Courchene, Foreword to *Wahbung: Our Tomorrows*

Warren Cariou and Niigaanwewidam James Sinclair, eds., *Manitowapow: Aboriginal Writings from the Land of Water* (Winnipeg: Highwater Press, 2011), 127.

## 1977 Grand Chief John Kelly, We Are All in the Ojibway Circle

Grand Chief John Kelly, "We Are All in the Ojibway Circle: Testimony Before the Royal Commission on the Northern Environment," cited in Michael Ondaatje, *From Ink Lake: Canadian Stories Selected by Michael Ondaatje* (Toronto: Vintage Canada, 1995), 579.

## 1996 A Word from Commissioners, The Royal Commission on Aboriginal Peoples

*A Word from Commissioners, People to People, Nation to Nation: Highlights from the Report of the Royal Commission on Aboriginal Peoples, 1996,* by Co-Chairs René Dussault, j.c.a., Georges Erasmus, and Commissioners Paul L.A.H. Chartrand, J. Peter Meekison, Viola Robinson, Mary Sillett, Bertha Wilson (Ottawa: Aboriginal and Northern Development Canada, 1996), 4.

# NOTES

**2000 Leroy Little Bear, Jagged Worldviews Colliding**
Marie Battiste, *Reclaiming Indigenous Voice and Vision* (Vancouver: UBC Press, 2000), 77.

**2003 Chief Joseph Gosnell of the Nisga'a, Speaking at Harvard**
Chief Joseph Gosnell, "A First Nation, Again: The Return of Self-Government and Self-Reliance in Canada's Nisga'a Nation" (speech, Harvard University, March 3, 2003).

**2005 Taiaiake Alfred, *Wasáse: Indigenous Pathways of Action and Freedom***
Taiaiake Alfred, *Wasáse: Indigenous Pathways of Action and Freedom* (Peterborough: Broadview Press, 2005), 13.

**2006 Jim Dumont, Indigenous Intelligence**
Jim Dumont, "Indigenous Intelligence" (lecture, University of Sudbury, October 18, 2006). "Indigenous Intelligence," directed by Daniel Moncion (October 18, 2006) [Video recording, DVD].

**2009 Siila Watt-Cloutier, Returning Canada to a Path of Principle**
Siila Watt-Cloutier, "Returning Canada to a Path of Principle," LaFontaine–Baldwin Symposium, Iqaluit, May 29, 2009.

**2011 E. Richard Atleo (Umeek), *Principles of Tsawalk: An Indigenous Approach to Global Crisis***
E. Richard Atleo (Umeek), *Principles of Tsawalk* (Vancouver: UBC Press, 2011).

**2012 Wab Kinew, Idle No More Is Not Just an "Indian Thing"**
Wab Kinew, "Idle No More Is Not Just an Indian Thing," in *The Winter We Danced*, The Kino-nda-niimi Collective, ed. (Winnipeg: ARP Books, 2014), 95. Originally appeared in *The Huffington Post*, December 17, 2012.

# NOTES

**2013 Jean Teillet, On the Manitoba Métis Victory**
Jean Teillet, "Taking Stock After MMF" (speech, Métis Nation of Ontario's 20th Annual General Assembly, Ottawa, August 24, 2013).

**2013 Chair Kathryn Teneese, On Reconciliation and Modernity**
Kathryn Teneese, "On Reconciliation and Modernity" (extract from speech, Salmon Festival, Revelstoke, British Columbia, September 28, 2013).

**2013 Niigaanwewidam James Sinclair, The Words We Have Inherited**
Niigaanwewidam James Sinclair, "The Words We Have Inherited," in *The Winter We Danced*, The Kino-nda-niimi Collective, ed. (Winnipeg: ARP Books, 2014), 271. Originally appeared in *The Winnipeg Free Press*, January 24, 2013.

# ACKNOWLEDGMENTS

First, to Roberto Alvarez, who has helped in every way, devoting himself to the book. I am grateful for his imagination and ability to make things happen.

And to Michael Reyes, who brought his enthusiasm and energy to the project; to Alain Pescador, who has been such a support; Andrew Lusztyk, who was there in the beginning; to Aidan Denison for pitching in whenever needed.

A special thanks to Brittany Lavery, who has done a wonderful job digging out photographs and helping to make them an important part of the argument in *The Comeback*.

I am very grateful to everyone who has permitted me to reproduce their work in Other People's Words: many thanks to Leroy Little Bear, Chief Joseph Gosnell, Taiaiake Alfred, Jim Dumont, Siila Watt-Cloutier, E. Richard Atleo (Umeek), Wab Kinew, Jean Teillet, Kathryn Teneese and Niigaanwewidam James Sinclair.

Many of them have also given me advice and ideas over the years. So a second thank you.

But also to Shawn A-in-chut Atleo, Ovide Mercredi, Romeo Saganash, Mark Podlasy, Roberta Jamieson, Clint Davis, J.P. Gladu, Mary Simon, Gerald McMaster, Jeannette Armstrong, Kent Monkman, Joseph Boyden, Connie Leonard of the TK'emlups (Kamloops) Indian Band, Michael DeGagné, Thomas King, Sakej Youngblood Henderson, Priscilla Settee, Hayden King, Jeff Hewitt, David Arnot, Catherine Odora Hoppers, Ric Young, Ryan van der Marel, Laurie McLaren of Nippissing, Kirt Ejesiak, Jesse Nicholas of the Ktunaxa Nation Council, Jenny Kay Dupuis, Gerry Woodman and David Wawryk of The Winnipeg Rifles, Catherine Precourt of the City of Stonewall, Terry Lusty of *Alberta Native News*, Tim Lewis and Lloyd Axworthy. And many thanks to Colm and Donna Feore.

In memory of Patrick Doyle who helped so many others.

I am often late, but everyone at Penguin stays calm. My best to Diane Turbide, who has been so helpful on *The Comeback*, along with Justin Stoller and, again Brittany Lavery, Beth Lockley, Tricia Van Der Grient, Mary Opper, David Ross, Karen Alliston and, of course, Nicole Winstanley.

Finally, to Ian, Jen, Eric and Hailey McCron; and to Chris Holmes and everyone at Moon River Marine, all of whom make writing on an off-the-grid Georgian Bay island so easy.

And, of course, Adrienne.

# INDEX